Supplem

to accompany

The **Holt** Handbook

Sixth Edition

Supplementary Exercises
to accompany

The **Holt**
Handbook

Sixth Edition

SCOTT DOUGLASS

Chattanooga State Technical

Community College

HEINLE & HEINLE

THOMSON LEARNING

Australia • Canada • Mexico • Singapore • Spain
United Kingdom • United States

ISBN: 0-15-506624-2

For more information about our products, contact us at:
Thomson Learning Academic Resource Center
1-800-423-0563

For permission to use material from this text, contact us by:
Phone: 1-800-730-2214
Fax: 1-800-730-2215
Web: http://www.thomsonrights.com

Asia
Thomson Learning
60 Albert Street, #15-01
Albert Complex
Singapore 189969

Australia
Nelson Thomson Learning
102 Dodds Street
South Melbourne, Victoria 3205
Australia

Canada
Nelson Thomson Learning
1120 Birchmount Road
Toronto, Ontario M1K 5G4
Canada

Europe/Middle East/Africa
Thomson Learning
Berkshire House
168-173 High Holborn
London WC1 V7AA
United Kingdom

Latin America
Thomson Learning
Seneca, 53
Colonia Polanco
11560 Mexico D.F.
Mexico

Spain
Paraninfo Thomson Learning
Calle/Magallanes, 25
28015 Madrid, Spain

Contents

Chapter 1   Exercise A
Getting Started

Consider a movie that you have recently enjoyed.

1. How would each of the following writing situations affect the content, style, organization, tone, and emphasis of an essay about this movie?

    •   A journal entry recording your informal impressions of the movie

    •   An examination question that asks you to summarize the movie's main idea

    •   A movie review for a composition class in which you evaluate both the movie's strengths and its weaknesses

    •   A letter to your local school board in which you try to convince your readers that, regardless of the movie's style or content, it should not be banned from the local public elementary schools

    •   An editorial for your school newspaper in which you try to persuade other students that the movie is not worth viewing

2. Choose one of the writing situations listed in number 1. On a separate sheet of paper, write an opening paragraph for the chosen assignment.

Chapter 1   Exercise B
Determining Your Purpose

Consider an essay subject you have chosen or your instructor has assigned. How will your purpose and audience affect what you write and how your write?

1. Name your subject.

_____

2. What is your purpose?

_____

_____

3. Who is your audience?

_____

4. What will you write and how will you write?

_____

_____

5. On a separate sheet of paper, write your first paragraph.

Chapter 1   **Exercise C**
Journal Entry

Write a journal entry evaluating your progress so far. Which of the strategies for finding something to write worked best for you? Why?

_____

_____

_____

_____

_____

_____

_____

_____

_____

Chapter 1   Exercise D
Freewriting

Begin with the most important sentence or idea in the paragraph you wrote in Exercise B, number 5. Freewrite until you have filled this page. If you wish, continue to freewrite on a separate sheet of paper.

_____

_____

_____

_____

_____

_____

_____

_____

_____

_____

Chapter 1   Exercise E
Brainstorming

Consider what you have discovered in Exercises B, C, and D. Do you
need to change any part of your plan for your essay?

1. Name your subject.

_____

2. What is your purpose?

_____

_____

3. Who is your audience?

_____

4. List all the points you can think of that seem pertinent to your
   essay.

_____

_____

_____

Chapter 1   Exercise F
Making a Cluster Diagram

Review the work you did for Exercises B–E. Use this material to help you construct a cluster diagram in the space below. This exercise should help you visualize how the ideas you have discovered can be organized into related groups.

Chapter 2   Exercise A
Making a Topic Tree

Review the work you did for Chapter 1 (Exercises B–E and the Cluster Diagram in Exercise F). Use this material to help you construct a topic tree in the space below. This exercise should help you visualize how the ideas you have discovered can be organized into related groups.

Chapter 2   Exercise B
Stating a Thesis

In the space provided below, formulate a clearly worded thesis statement for each of the following topics.

1. A person who has profoundly influenced the course of your life

_____

_____

_____

_____

2. Preparing for your retirement

_____

_____

_____

_____

Chapter 2   Exercise C
Stating a Thesis

In the space provided below, formulate a clearly worded thesis statement for each of the following topics.

1. Public funding of the arts

_____

_____

_____

_____

2. The value of a college education

_____

_____

_____

_____

Chapter 2   Exercise D
Stating a Thesis

In the space provided below, formulate a clearly worded thesis statement for each of the following topics.

1. The role of cultural diversity

_____

_____

_____

_____

2. Political correctness and the First Amendment

_____

_____

_____

_____

Chapter 2   Exercise E
Stating a Thesis

Review the topic tree you made in Exercise A. Use it to help you develop a thesis for an essay. Write your thesis in the space below.

_____

_____

_____

_____

_____

_____

_____

_____

_____

Chapter 2   Exercise F
Preparing an Informal Outline

After reviewing your notes, prepare an informal outline for a paper on
the thesis you developed in Exercise E.

_____

_____

_____

_____

_____

_____

_____

_____

_____

_____

Chapter 3   Exercise A
Writing a Rough Draft

Write a rough draft of the essay you have been planning. In the space provided, begin your rough draft. Then use your own paper to complete the rough draft.

_____

_____

_____

_____

_____

_____

_____

_____

_____

_____

Chapter 3   Exercise B
Collaborative Revision

After you have drafted a paper, form teams of two or three for collaborative revision. Read each other's papers and write responses to the questions below. Then discuss the comments.

- What is the essay about? Is the topic suitable for this assignment?

- What is the main point of the essay? Is the thesis stated? If so, is it clearly worded? If not, how can the wording be improved? Is the thesis stated in an appropriate location?

- Is the essay arranged logically? Do the body paragraphs appear in an appropriate order?

- What ideas support the thesis? Does each body paragraph develop one of these?

- Does each body paragraph have a unifying idea? Are topic sentences needed to summarize the information in the paragraphs? Are the topic sentences clearly related to the thesis?

- Is any necessary information missing? Identify any areas that seem to need further development. Is any information irrelevant? If so, indicate possible deletions.

- Can you contribute anything to the essay? Can you offer any ideas or examples from your own reading, experience, or observations that would strengthen the writer's points?

- Can you follow the writer's ideas? If not, would clearer connections between sentences or paragraphs be helpful? If so, where are such connections needed?

- Is the introductory paragraph interesting to you? Would another kind of introduction work better?

- Does the conclusion leave you with a sense of completion? Would another kind of conclusion be more appropriate?

- Is anything unclear or confusing?

- What is the essay's chief strength? What is its chief weakness?

Chapter 4   Exercise A
Writer's Notebook: Composing an Essay

Prepare a personalized list of the most important considerations as you choose a topic.

1. _____

2. _____

3. _____

4. _____

Prepare a personalized list of the most important considerations as you create a cluster diagram or a topic tree.

1. _____

2. _____

3. _____

4. _____

Chapter 4   Exercise B
Writer's Notebook: Composing an Essay

Prepare a personalized list of the most important considerations as you compose a thesis statement.

1. _____

2. _____

3. _____

4. _____

Prepare a personalized list of the most important considerations as you prepare the final draft.

1. _____

2. _____

3. _____

4. _____

Name _____ Date _____ Score _____

Chapter 5   Exercise A
Essay Patterns and Purposes

Compose an introductory paragraph that includes a clear thesis statement to serve as part of a cause-and-effect essay. If necessary, use your own paper to complete this exercise.

Topic for this cause-and-effect essay:

a morning that you slept through your alarm

_____

_____

_____

_____

_____

_____

_____

_____

Chapter 5   Exercise B
Essay Patterns and Purposes

Compose an introductory paragraph that includes a clear thesis statement to serve as part of a comparison-and-contrast essay. If necessary, use your own paper to complete this exercise.

Topic for this comparison-and-contrast essay:

two colleges you considered attending

_____

_____

_____

_____

_____

_____

_____

_____

_____

Chapter 6   Exercise A
Patterns of Paragraph Development

Determine one possible method of development for a paragraph on each of these topics. Then, in the space below, write a paragraph on one of the topics.

1. Depending on friends for transportation

2. An unexpected bill for automobile repairs

3. A perfect spot to take a vacation

4. Troubles that accompany being computer illiterate

5. The ideal campsite

_____

_____

_____

_____

_____

_____

_____

Chapter 6   Exercise B
Patterns of Paragraph Development

Determine one possible method of development for a paragraph on each of these topics. Then, in the space below, write a paragraph on one of the topics.

1. The most useful software titles

2. The perils of not backing up computer files

3. The benefits of extracurricular activities

4. Jobs to avoid

5. The types of people who go to concerts

_____

_____

_____

_____

_____

_____

_____

Chapter 6   Exercise C
Well-Developed Paragraphs

Read the following paragraph and then answer these questions.

1. In general terms, how could the paragraph be developed further?

_____

_____

2. What pattern of development might be used?

_____

_____

Civility once was considered the cornerstone of a progressive society. Disagreements were noted, but seldom publicly acknowledged. Violation of this custom among certain classes often resulted in the practice of dueling, which acted as a deterrent to uncivil behavior because of the finality of the outcome. Although dueling is now outlawed in our society, many disagreements are still settled through violence. Lack of civility remains problematic in our society.

Chapter 6   Exercise D
Well-Developed Paragraphs

Read the following paragraph and then answer these questions.

1. In general terms, how could the paragraph be developed further?

_____

_____

2. What pattern of development might be used?

_____

_____

Amish Friendship Bread is a culinary treat. It begins with the receipt of a gift of a batch of starter batter. The entire process—from receiving the batter to the finished product—takes ten days. The first day requires the addition of flour, milk, and sugar. Days two through five involve the once-a-day, gentle mixing of the batter. On day six, more milk, flour, and sugar are added. Days seven through nine repeat the daily mixing. On day ten, the long-anticipated outcome is realized as a portion of the batter is baked into a succulent loaf, while saving a starter batch to share with a friend.

Chapter 7   Exercise A
Thinking Critically

Compose a brief argument that incorporates obvious examples of bias through slanted language, tone, and choice of evidence. Be as creative as you consider appropriate.

_____

_____

_____

_____

_____

_____

_____

_____

_____

_____

Chapter 7   Exercise B
Thinking Critically

Revise the argument that you composed in Exercise A, eliminating the examples of bias to produce a well-written piece that reflects your critical thinking skills.

_____

_____

_____

_____

_____

_____

_____

_____

_____

_____

Chapter 8   Exercise A
Thinking Logically

Compose a brief argument that incorporates three logical fallacies mentioned in the list below. Be as creative as you consider appropriate.

hasty generalization   argument to the person
red herring   begging the question
either/or fallacy   *post hoc* fallacy

_____

_____

_____

_____

_____

_____

_____

_____

_____

Chapter 8   Exercise B
Thinking Logically

Revise the argument that you composed in Exercise A, eliminating the
logical fallacies.

_____

_____

_____

_____

_____

_____

_____

_____

_____

_____

Chapter 9   Exercise A
Writing an Argumentative Essay

List four arguments in favor of and four arguments against the following
statement.

Cyclists should be permitted to ride on highways.

For

1. _____

2. _____

3. _____

4. _____

Against

1. _____

2. _____

3. _____

4. _____

Chapter 9   Exercise B
Writing an Argumentative Essay

List four arguments in favor of and four arguments against the following statement.

> Downloading music via the Internet should not be regulated by the government.

For

1. _____

2. _____

3. _____

4. _____

Against

1. _____

2. _____

3. _____

4. _____

Review Exercise A for Part 1, Chapters 1–6
Writing Essays and Paragraphs

In the space provided, add further development to the ideas presented in the following paragraph. If you need additional space, complete the assignment on your own paper.

    Most people look forward to vacations with great eagerness. Where they vacation, however, differs widely. Vacation locations depend on such factors as personal preference, financial considerations, and time available. Some people look forward to spending a few days in the mountains, while others can think of nothing more pleasant than sunning on a sugar-white beach. Regardless of the destination, a vacation remains the goal and basis of fond memories for nearly everyone.

_____

_____

_____

_____

_____

_____

_____

Name _____ Date _____ Score _____

Review Exercise B for Part 1, Chapters 1–6
Writing Essays and Paragraphs

In the space provided, add further development to the ideas presented in the following paragraph. If you need additional space, complete the assignment on your own paper.

   Young adults are social creatures. They enjoy gathering with others their age to celebrate various types of occasions. For example, an overnight tailgate party may precede a football game, or a group may gather for a clambake on a beach, or spring break may demand a special celebration. No matter the type of gathering, attention must be paid to details in order to make the celebration memorable.

_____

_____

_____

_____

_____

_____

_____

Review Exercise C for Part 1, Chapters 7–9
Critical Thinking and Argumentation

In the space below, create your own version of an argument based on insufficient supporting evidence. As the topic for this paragraph, take a stance regarding the role that television has played in the pattern of declining scores on reading comprehension tests during the past twenty-five years.

_____

_____

_____

_____

_____

_____

_____

_____

_____

_____

Review Exercise D for Part 1, Chapters 7–9
Critical Thinking and Argumentation

Develop an argument on the same topic prescribed in Exercise C, but provide the necessary supporting evidence to convince your reader to accept your position.

_____

_____

_____

_____

_____

_____

_____

_____

_____

Chapter 10   Exercise A
The Research Process

The following schedule will not only give you an overview of the research process, but it will also help you manage your time.

Activity	*Date Due*	*Date Completed*
Choose a Topic (10a)	_____	_____
Map Out a Search Strategy (10b)	_____	_____
Do Exploratory Research and Formulate a Research Question (10c)	_____	_____
Assemble a Working Bibliography (10d)	_____	_____
Develop a Tentative Thesis (10e)	_____	_____
Do Focused Research (10f)	_____	_____
Take Notes (10g)	_____	_____
Decide On a Thesis (10h)	_____	_____
Prepare a Formal Outline (10i)	_____	_____
Write a Rough Draft (10j)	_____	_____
Revise Your Drafts (10k)	_____	_____
Prepare a Final Draft (10l)	_____	_____

Chapter 10   Exercise B
Moving from Assignment to Topic

List five subjects you want to know more about.

1. _____

2. _____

3. _____

4. _____

5. _____

Name _____ Date _____ Score _____

Chapter 10   Exercise C
Moving from Assignment to Topic

For each of the following, base your response on the list you created in Exercise B. Identify the subject by citing its corresponding number as it appears in Exercise B.

1. Which subject would be most interesting for you to do research and write about? Why?

#_____ _____

_____

_____

2. Which subject would be most interesting for your audience to read about? Why?

#_____ _____

_____

_____

3. Which subject would best lend itself to the assignment you have been given? How?

#_____ _____

_____

Chapter 10   Exercise D
Moving from Assignment to Topic

For each of the following, base your response on the list you created in Exercise B. Identify the subject by citing its corresponding number as it appears in Exercise B.

1. For which of these subjects would you
    be able to locate the best source material?   #_____

2. Which subject do you choose? Why?

#___ _____

    _____

    _____

3. In the form of a question, record what you hope to find out by
    doing research and writing about this subject.

    _____

    _____

    _____

Chapter 10   Exercise E
Mapping Out a Search Strategy

List the reference books, bibliographies, periodicals, indexes, databases, and other resources that are related to your subject and available to you. Add to this list as you make discoveries in the course of your research and writing. Be sure to record all the information you will need for documenting your sources.

_____

_____

_____

_____

_____

_____

_____

_____

_____

Name _____ Date _____ Score _____

Chapter 10   Exercise F
Mapping Out a Search Strategy

Search the resources that you identified in Exercise E. List the books, articles, people, organizations, and other material that you think will be most useful to you. Write a brief note to help you remember what you hope to learn or gain from each source. What do you expect each source to contribute to your research and paper? Revise this list as you continue to locate and evaluate source material. (Look ahead to the exercises for Chapter 11.) Be sure to record all information you will need for documenting your sources.

_____

_____

_____

_____

_____

_____

_____

_____

Chapter 11   Exercise A
Evaluating Library Sources

Select one of the resources (book, essay, or article from a newspaper, magazine, or journal) that you have identified in Chapter 10 Exercise E, and then analyze its usefulness to your purposes.

1. What types of materials are used?

_____

_____

_____

2. Does the writer use more direct quotations than paraphrases? Are you able to determine why? If so, explain.

_____

_____

3. How does the writer give the reader a sense of the source's validity or credibility?

_____

_____

_____

Chapter 11   Exercise B
Evaluating Library Sources

Select another of the resources (book, essay, or article from a newspaper, magazine, or journal) that you have identified in Chapter 10 Exercise E, and then analyze its usefulness to your purposes. (This repeats Exercise A, but with a second source.)

1. What types of materials are used?

_____

_____

2. Does the writer use more direct quotations than paraphrases? Are you able to determine why? If so, explain.

_____

_____

3. How does the writer give the reader a sense of the source's validity or credibility?

_____

_____

_____

Name _____ Date _____ Score _____

Chapter 12   Exercise A
Conducting a Keyword Search

For this exercise, select one of the search engines mentioned in Chapter 12 (section b) in *The Holt Handbook*. Choose a topic that interests you, and conduct a keyword search. Revise the keywords as necessary to obtain a manageable list of documents. Select one document, and then respond to these questions. Print at least the first screen of the Web site you select.

1. What is the source of the information?

_____

2. Is the Web master identified? Do you have reason to consider this author credible and reliable? Explain.

_____

3. Does the site mention when it was last updated? If so, record it.

_____

4. Does the text adhere to the conventions of research material that would be expected from print material? If so, briefly describe how the document meets those conventions. If not, what is lacking?

_____

5. Briefly evaluate the graphics, sound, or video. Are they used to enhance the text, or do they mask a lack of solid content?

_____

Chapter 12   Exercise B
Conducting a Keyword Search

Repeat Exercise A using a different search engine. Select from the search engines mentioned in Chapter 12 (section b) in *The Holt Handbook*. Using the same keyword as you used in Exercise A, conduct a keyword search. Select one document, and then respond to these questions. Print at least the first screen of the Web site you select. Compare the information gathered in Exercises A and B.

1. What is the source of the information?

_____

2. Is the Web master identified? Do you have reason to consider this author credible and reliable? Explain.

_____

3. Does the site mention when it was last updated? If so, record it.

_____

4. Does the text adhere to the conventions of research material that would be expected from print material? If so, briefly describe how the document meets those conventions. If not, what is lacking?

_____

5. Briefly evaluate the graphics, sound, or video. Are they used to enhance the text, or do they mask a lack of solid content?

_____

Chapter 12   Exercise C
Using the Internet for Research

For this exercise, use one of the subjects that you identified in Chapter 10 Exercise B. Working with the search engine that you prefer, conduct a keyword search.

1. Estimate the total number of responses the search engine yields.

_____

2. How does this number of responses compare to the number of resources that you listed in Chapter 10 Exercises E and F?

_____

_____

3. Select a specific item on the list provided by the search engine's results. Summarize the effort required of you to consult this item.

_____

_____

4. If you encountered any difficulties as you used the search engine, note them so you can avoid them later.

_____

_____

Chapter 12   Exercise D
Using the Internet for Research

1. List three advantages that you consider Internet research offers over traditional research methods in a library.

    a. _____

    b. _____

    c. _____

2. List three potential hazards for those who depend exclusively on Internet research.

    a. _____

    b. _____

    c. _____

3. On which method of research—library or Internet—will you likely depend as you complete your next research paper? Explain your reasons.

    _____

    _____

Name _____ Date _____ Score _____

Chapter 13   Exercise A
Evaluating Web Sites

Using the Web browser and search engine that you prefer, locate a Web site that strikes you as interesting. Answer the following questions as a method of evaluating the Web site. Also, print at least the first screen of the Web site.

1. Does the site include a list of Contents that tells you the general topics? If so, what are the general topics?

   _____

   _____

2. Scroll to the bottom of the home page to locate the person responsible for managing the site (often referred to as the "Web master.") Is a name mentioned on this site?

   _____

3. Does the site mention when it was last updated? If so, record it.

   _____

4. Click on links to browse through the site. Is navigation easy? Is the site's organization easily understood?

   _____

Chapter 13   Exercise B
Evaluating Web Sites

Using the Web browser and search engine that you prefer, complete the following tasks to help you evaluate a source that you locate on the Internet.

Type in: **Sistine Chapel**

1. How many documents are found? _____

2. How are the listed documents sorted? (usually by relevance or site)

_____

3. Are any of the listed documents commercial? (Are they basically advertisements for a publisher, textbook, tour guide, or airline?)

_____

4. Are any of the listed documents unrelated to the Sistine Chapel? If so, estimate the percentage.

_____

Chapter 13   Exercise C
Citing Electronic Sources

Consult Chapter 16 ("MLA Documentation") of *The Holt Handbook* and use proper MLA documentation format for electronic sources to complete the following task.

1. Cite the source you used in Chapter 13, Exercise A: Evaluating Web Sites.

_____

_____

_____

2. Cite the source you used in Chapter 13, Exercise B: Evaluating Web Sites.

_____

_____

_____

Chapter 13   Exercise D
Citing Electronic Sources

Consult Chapter 16 ("MLA Documentation") of *The Holt Handbook* and use proper MLA documentation format for electronic sources to complete the following task. (This exercise repeats Exercise C, but uses information gathered in the exercises for Chapter 12.)

1. Cite the source you used in Chapter 12, Exercise A: Conducting a Keyword Search.

_____

_____

_____

_____

2. Cite the source you used in Chapter 12, Exercise B: Conducting a Keyword Search.

_____

_____

_____

Chapter 14   Exercise A
Summarizing

Complete the following tasks based on one of these debatable issues:

   a)   The federal minimum wage for all restaurant employees

   b)   Smoking on domestic airline flights

1.   Write a one-sentence summary of your own position on the issue.
     (Include reasons that support the position.)

     _____

     _____

     _____

2.   Write a one-sentence summary of your friend's position on the
     same issue. (Include reasons that support the position.)

     _____

     _____

     _____

Chapter 14   Exercise B
Paraphrasing and Quoting

Using a search engine, locate a source that discusses the issue you selected in Exercise A. Compose a paraphrase of the author's position. Provide a printout or photocopy of the portion of the source on which you base your paraphrase.

_____

_____

_____

_____

_____

Provide one sentence that paraphrases one aspect of the author's position, and include a quotation that features distinctive phrases.

_____

_____

_____

_____

Chapter 14   Exercise C
Summarizing

Complete the following tasks based on one of these debatable issues:

c) Public service instead of jail time for first-time drug offenders

d) Cell phone use by drivers

1. Write a one-sentence summary of your own position on the issue. (Include reasons that support the position.)

_____

_____

_____

2. Write a one-sentence summary of your friend's position on the same issue. (Include reasons that support the position.)

_____

_____

_____

Chapter 14   Exercise D
Paraphrasing and Quoting

Using a search engine, locate a source that discusses the issue you selected in Exercise C. Compose a paraphrase of the author's position. Provide a printout or photocopy of the portion of the source on which you base your paraphrase. (This exercise repeats Exercise B, but with different topic options.)

_____

_____

_____

_____

_____

Provide one sentence that paraphrases one aspect of the author's position, and include a quotation that features distinctive phrases.

_____

_____

_____

Chapter 15   Exercise A
Avoiding Plagiarism

1. In the space below, copy the paraphrase you wrote for Chapter 14 Exercise B, inserting the necessary MLA-style parenthetical citation(s) of source material.

_____

_____

_____

_____

_____

_____

2. In the space below, write the entry you would use for this source on your MLA-style Works Cited page.

_____

_____

_____

Chapter 15   Exercise B
Avoiding Plagiarism

1. In the space below, copy the paraphrase you wrote for Chapter 14 Exercise D, inserting the necessary MLA-style parenthetical citation(s) of source material.

_____

_____

_____

_____

_____

_____

2. In the space below, write the entry you would use for this source on your MLA-style Works Cited page.

_____

_____

_____

Chapter 16   Exercise A
MLA Documentation

For each of the following types of sources, provide a bibliographic entry that complies with MLA documentation guidelines.

A book by two authors

_____

_____

_____

An edited book

_____

_____

_____

An article in a monthly magazine

_____

_____

_____

Chapter 16   Exercise B
MLA Documentation

For each of the following types of sources, provide a bibliographic entry that complies with MLA documentation guidelines.

A signed article in a newspaper

_____

_____

_____

A non-periodical publication on CD-ROM (such as Encarta®)

_____

_____

_____

A Web page

_____

_____

_____

Chapter 17   Exercise A
APA and Other Documentation Styles

For each of the following types of sources, provide a bibliographic entry that complies with APA documentation guidelines.

A book by two authors

_____

_____

_____

An edited book

_____

_____

_____

An article in a monthly magazine

_____

_____

_____

A signed article in a newspaper

_____

_____

_____

Chapter 17   Exercise B
APA and Other Documentation Styles

For each of the following types of sources, provide a bibliographic entry that complies with CMS documentation guidelines.

A book by two authors

_____

_____

_____

An edited book

_____

_____

_____

An article in a monthly magazine

_____

_____

_____

A signed article in a newspaper

_____

_____

_____

Chapter 18   Exercise A
Research Notebook: A Student's Process

Respond to each of the following based on current plans to write a researched essay. If you don't have one currently underway, respond based on a recent experience in writing a researched essay.

1. Identify the topic for this essay.

_____

2. If the topic was assigned to you, are you comfortable with it? Explain your response.

_____

_____

_____

3. If you chose the topic, were any limitations placed on your selection? Are you comfortable with these restrictions? Have you found that some limitations might be useful?

_____

_____

_____

Name _____ Date _____ Score _____

Chapter 18   Exercise B
Research Notebook: A Student's Process

Respond to each of the following based on current plans to write a researched essay. If you don't have one currently underway, respond based on a recent experience in writing a researched essay.

1. Provide three points that you have found useful for incorporating source material into an essay.

a. _____

_____

b. _____

_____

c. _____

_____

2. Identify two people on whom you could depend to provide helpful and constructive advice about your essay immediately prior to preparing the final draft for submission. Explain their qualifications.

a. _____

b. _____

Review Exercise A for Part 2, Chapters 10–18
Research

In the space below, record five points with which you were familiar as
you began this research unit, but which became more helpful after you
completed the exercises for Chapters 10–18.

1. _____

_____

2. _____

_____

3. _____

_____

4. _____

_____

5. _____

_____

Review Exercise B for Part 2, Chapters 10–18
Research

In the space below, record five points that were entirely new to you when you began this research unit, but now (after completing the exercises for Chapters 10–18) you realize that they have merit and will likely prove helpful as you complete your next research assignment.

1. _____

_____

2. _____

_____

3. _____

_____

4. _____

_____

5. _____

_____

Review Exercise C for Part 2, Chapters 12–13
Research

In the space below, record five points that you've found especially helpful and that you would offer as recommendations to someone new to the Internet.

1. _____

_____

2. _____

_____

3. _____

_____

4. _____

_____

5. _____

_____

Review Exercise D for Part 2, Chapters 12–13
Research

In the space below, record five problem areas that you've encountered related to the Internet and that you would encourage others to avoid.

1. _____

_____

2. _____

_____

3. _____

_____

4. _____

_____

5. _____

_____

Name _____ Date _____ Score _____

Review Exercise E for Part 2, Chapter 16
MLA Documentation

The following notes identify sources in a paper on censorship and the Internet. Following the proper format for MLA Documentation, create a bibliographic entry for each source.

1. An essay by Nat Hentoff titled "Speech Should Not Be Limited" on pages 22–26 of the book *Censorship: Opposing Viewpoints,* edited by Terry O'Neill. Greenhaven Press in St. Paul, Minnesota, publishes the book. The publication year is 1985.

   _____

   _____

   _____

2. "If You Don't Love It, Leave It," an essay by Esther Dyson in the *New York Times Magazine,* July 15, 1995, on pages 26 and 27.

   _____

   _____

   _____

Review Exercise F for Part 2, Chapter 16
MLA Documentation

The following notes identify sources in a paper on censorship and the Internet. Following the proper format for MLA Documentation, create a bibliographic entry for each source.

1. Terry O'Neill's introduction to *Censorship: Opposing Viewpoints,* found on pages 13 and 14. Greenhaven Press in St. Paul, Minnesota, publishes the book. The publication year is 1985.

_____

_____

_____

2. An essay in the *Village Voice* titled "The Speech Police Invade Cyberspace" by Nat Hentoff. It was published on July 11, 1995, on pages 22 and 23.

_____

_____

_____

Chapter 19   Exercise A
Sentence Review

Expand each basic sentence by adding at least a phrase or a clause.

Example: George bought a car.
            George bought a car that he will pick up Monday.

1. The dog barked.

    _____

2. Sarah bought a house.

    _____

3. I will finish my homework.

    _____

4. The food is cooked.

    _____

5. Dr. Shuster will be back Tuesday.

    _____

6. My brother called.

    _____

Chapter 19   Exercise B
Sentence Review

Expand each basic sentence by adding at least a phrase or a clause.

Example: George bought a car.
              George bought a car that he will pick up Monday.

1. We began our vacation.

    _____

2. Camille rode the trolley.

    _____

3. When did Stacey leave?

    _____

4. The library is closed.

    _____

5. Sarah swam a dozen laps.

    _____

6. John played the violin.

    _____

Chapter 19   Exercise C
Simple Sentences

In the space provided, write "S" if the example has a subject or "X" if it does not. Underline the simple subject that you find. If the sentence is not complete, use the space provided to convert the fragment to a simple sentence.

Example: __X__ Liked my new car.

All of my soccer teammates liked my new car. _____

1. _____ More than you will ever know.

_____

2. _____ Forty chairs per classroom.

_____

3. _____ The scouts played cards until after midnight.

_____

4. _____ Need several pounds of shrimp.

_____

5. _____ Meg cares about her patients.

_____

Chapter 19   Exercise D
Simple Sentences

In the space provided, write "S" if the example has a subject or "X" if it does not. Underline the simple subject that you find. If the sentence is not complete, use the space provided to convert the fragment to a simple sentence.

Example: __X__ Liked my new car.

All of my soccer teammates liked my new car. _____

1. _____ Comprehension and vocabulary.

_____

2. _____ Beyond his limit, Brian took a break.

_____

3. _____ Is running several miles each morning.

_____

4. _____ Love going to the mall.

_____

5. _____ Our vacation was refreshing.

_____

Chapter 20   Exercise A
Building Compound Sentences

Combine each of the following pairs of simple sentences to form compound sentences. Use any of the following elements as you complete this exercise: coordinating conjunction, transitional words or phrases, correlative conjunctions, semicolons, or colons.

Example:

The scouts played cards until after midnight.
They were not much help with breaking camp this morning.

The scouts played cards until after midnight, so they were not much help with breaking camp this morning.

1. Erica pitched a no-hitter. Her team won the championship game.

   _____

   _____

2. My best friend is my dog. Her best friend is a delicious bone.

   _____

3. Mr. Adamson often misplaces his glasses. Mrs. Adamson keeps a spare pair handy.

   _____

   _____

Chapter 20   Exercise B
Building Complex Sentences

Use a subordinating conjunction or relative pronoun to combine each of the following groups of sentences into one well-constructed complex sentence.

Example:

The scouts played cards until after midnight.
They were not much help with breaking camp this morning.

<u>Because the scouts played cards until after midnight, they were not much help with breaking camp this morning.</u>

1. The coach presented the game ball to Angela. She hit the game-winning home run.

_____

_____

2. My best friend is my dog. Her best friend is a delicious bone.

_____

3. Mr. Adamson often forgets to record his checks in the checkbook. Mrs. Adamson has learned not to trust him.

_____

_____

Chapter 21   Exercise A
Writing Emphatic Sentences

The following paragraph has both active and passive verbs. On your own paper, rewrite the paragraph using only active verbs.

Conestoga wagons are generally associated with the western frontier, but they were first used in Pennsylvania around 1725. Because heavy supplies were carried well by the wagons, they were used by settlers during the movement west. When the wagons were grouped for traveling, they were called wagon trains. In this way, the plains were crossed safely by many migrants. After the 1850s, the wagons were replaced by the railroads.

Chapter 21   Exercise B
Writing Emphatic Sentences

The following paragraph has both active and passive verbs. On your own paper, rewrite the paragraph using only active verbs.

When a European coast was landed on by the Vikings, fear of the Vikings' sudden and fierce raids was learned by the inhabitants. Their high-powered boats were sailed by these Norsemen from Scandinavia to the continent or Britain. The ships were decorated with striped sails and colorful circular shields. Little brightness was brought to the raiders' victims by these ships. A permanent mark was left on the territories that were attacked and occupied with ferocity and persistence by the Vikings. Particularly influenced by their customs and language were Norman France and the region of the British "Danelaw."

Chapter 22   Exercise A
Writing Concise Sentences

On your own paper, rewrite the following paragraph to eliminate wordiness.

When he first began writing, Samuel Clemens incorporated his own experiences that he had had. At one time he worked as a riverboat pilot on the Mississippi River. The pseudonym that he used as a writer, "Mark Twain," came from his experience during those days. This phrase was called out to mark the two-fathom mark on the riverboat line. When the Civil War started, it closed the river. Clemens could no longer pilot riverboats, so he moved west and became a newspaper writer. From his experience as a riverboat pilot, he took along his literary name.

Chapter 22   Exercise B
Writing Concise Sentences

On your own paper, revise the following paragraph to eliminate any unnecessary repetition of words or ideas. Also revise to eliminate deadwood, utility words, or circumlocution.

The seven daughters of Atlas are known as the Pleiades. They were pursued by Orion. Orion was unable to seize any of them. Orion continued to follow them. Orion continued to follow them until Zeus took pity on them. Zeus placed them in the heavens. Seven stars make up the Pleiades constellation. Only six stars are clearly visible. The seventh is invisible except for some people. These people are those who have especially keen vision. In Greek mythology, the seventh star represented Electra. Electra was the mother of Dardanus. Dardanus founded the Trojan race. There is a legend about Electra. The legend held Electra dropped from the sky. Electra did not want to look down from the sky. Electra did not want to see the destruction of Troy. Today, though, all seven stars are visible in the Pleiades. Actually, more than seven stars can be seen. But you must use binoculars to see more than seven stars in this cluster. You can even see several hundred stars. But you must use a telescope. Viewing through a telescope will yield several hundred stars.

Chapter 22   Exercise C
Writing Concise Sentences

On your own paper, revise the rambling sentences in the following paragraph by eliminating excessive coordination and subordination, unnecessary use of the passive voice, and overuse of wordy prepositional phrases and noun constructions. As you revise, make your sentences more concise by deleting nonessential words and superfluous repetition.

Orion lost the trail of the Pleiades. Orion became the companion of Artemis. Artemis was a virgin goddess. Artemis was the goddess of the moon. Artemis was also the twin sister of Apollo. Apollo feared for his sister's chastity. Apollo sent a large scorpion to chase Orion. Orion observed the scorpion enter a body of water. Orion pursued the scorpion. Apollo then persuaded Artemis to shoot the object. The object was bobbing in the waves. Her arrow pierced Orion's head. Artemis was deeply saddened at her loss. Artemis placed Orion's image among the stars. In the stars, Orion's image continues to be stalked by the scorpion. The scorpion is also a constellation. Orion and the scorpion are separated. They are separated by a great distance. The Pleiades, however, are in front of Orion. Orion is much closer to the Pleiades. Orion continues to pursue the Pleiades.

Chapter 22   Exercise D
Writing Concise Sentences

Use sentence combining to rewrite the following paragraph in the space provided so that it is more concise and effective.

     Shakespeare had a source for *Macbeth*. The story came from another book. That book was Holinshed's *Chronicles*. There Shakespeare found the tale. He found an account of King Duncan's murder. There he found a suggestion about Lady Macbeth. She was ambitious. There was the story of how Macbeth rose. It also included how he fell.

_____

_____

_____

_____

_____

_____

_____

Chapter 23   Exercise A
Writing Varied Sentences

On your own paper, use coordination, subordination, and embedding to revise this string of choppy simple sentences into a more varied and interesting paragraph.

The Authorized Version of the Bible was first published in 1611. The Authorized Version of the Bible is often referred to as the King James Version. It involved several years of work by numerous scholars. Much of the year prior to its publication was devoted to final preparations. After it had been prepared, the document was sent to press. Many steps were taken during those final months. One step involved calling upon writers of the day. Several of the writers were eminent. They were needed to "refine" this translation. It was the most recent English translation. These writers devoted their efforts to the project. They enhanced the poetic qualities of Proverbs. They enhanced the poetic qualities of the Song of Solomon. And they enhanced the poetic qualities of the Psalms.

Chapter 23   Exercise B
Writing Varied Sentences

Complete each of the following steps on your own paper.

A. Combine each of the following sentence groups into one long
   sentence.
B. Then, compose a relatively short sentence to follow each long one.
C. Finally, combine all the sentences into a paragraph, adding any
   transitions necessary for coherence. Proofread your paragraph to be
   sure that the sentences are varied in length.

1. The King James Version of the Bible is the subject of many
   literary legends. One of the legends is intriguing. It alleges that
   Shakespeare's hand is present in the King James Version of the
   Bible. More specifically, though, it alleges that Shakespeare's
   hand is present in the 46th Psalm.

2. Count to the forty-sixth word from the beginning of the psalm.
   You will find that it is *shake*. Then identify the forty-sixth word
   from the end of the psalm. You will find that it is *spear*.

3. The situation becomes even more intriguing. It becomes even
   more intriguing when we realize that the revision work was
   underway in 1610. It becomes even more intriguing when we also
   realize that Shakespeare was forty-six years old in 1610.

Chapter 23   Exercise C
Writing Varied Sentences

On your own paper, revise the compound sentences in this passage so the sentence structure is varied and the writer's meaning and emphasis are clear.

Leonardo da Vinci's *The Last Supper* is one of the most easily recognized works of art. It was produced during Leonardo's residence in Milan. Leonardo was under the patronage of Duke Sforza. Leonardo used oil and tempera for *The Last Supper*. He used a wall in the refectory of Santa Maria della Grazie as his "canvas." Even the most casual art observer has viewed a copy of *The Last Supper*. But few serious students of art realize that it is actually a mural. It measures 14 ft. 5 in. x 28 ft.. It is surprising that Leonardo completed his work on such a large scale. It is surprising to many who have seen only small replicas. Many of these replicas are the size of a post card.

Chapter 23   Exercise D
Writing Varied Sentences

On your own paper, revise the compound sentences in this passage so the sentence structure is varied and the writer's meaning and emphasis are clear.

Giorgio Vasari records an interesting anecdote. Giorgio Vasari was an Italian art historian. He lived during the sixteenth century. The anecdote concerns Leonardo's use of models. These models were used for *The Last Supper*. Leonardo drew the disciples from life. Leonardo encountered difficulty in locating a suitable Judas Iscariot. While he worked on the painting, Leonardo met with some problems. Leonardo was troubled by the prior of Santa Maria. The prior monitored the work's progress. He monitored from a vantage uncomfortably close for Leonardo. The prior expressed his concerns to Duke Sforza. Leonardo heard that the prior had complained to the duke. Leonardo mentioned that any delay he had experienced was merely the result of his having encountered difficulty in identifying a model. The model was for the betrayer. Leonardo pointed out that he would be delayed no longer. He had located his model. The prior would serve nicely.

Name _____ Date _____ Score _____

Review Exercise A for Part 3, Chapters 19–23
Sentence Style

On your own paper, revise the following student draft to achieve greater sentence variety by varying the length, type, openings, and word order of the sentences.

A Cliffhanger

I slowly opened my eyes. I looked to my right. I could see the huge rocks. They lay awaiting a sacrifice fifty feet below. I looked to my left. I could see the questioning faces peering over the edge of the cliff. I could see snowflakes falling gently around me. Suddenly I came to a realization. Only one thing stood between the boulders and me. It was a gate. I came to another realization at that moment. I knew that skiing was not the sport for me.

It all happened one day in January. I had joined the school ski club. I still don't know why I had joined the ski club, but it seemed like a good opportunity to have fun and meet people. This was our first ski trip.

We rode on a bus to the ski lodge. The ride took an hour. During the ride, I began to worry. I wondered whether I would have been better off missing the trip altogether. I thought about everything that could possibly go wrong; I envisioned myself lying on a hospital bed. I envisioned doctors standing all around. They were trying to revive me. My friends had promised to teach me the basics of the sport. In spite of this, I could foresee a terrifying experience. I was right.

Review Exercise B for Part 3, Chapters 19–23
Sentence Style

This exercise includes a continuation of the student draft presented in Exercise A. On your own paper, revise these paragraphs to achieve greater sentence variety by varying the length, type, openings, and word order of the sentences.

    We finally reached the lodge. I decided to rationalize. I decided that this is skiing; it's supposed to be fun. I was then feeling a bit courageous. I chose to begin on the intermediate slope. I went to the top of the mountain. I looked down the icy terrain. Visions of survival soon faded. A friend offered a few words of encouragement, and I began to conquer the mountain. I went down piece by piece.

    I would ski about twenty feet at a time. Then I would stop. That way I would not pick up too much momentum. This process continued with healthy results. Then I reached one particularly demanding part of the slope. It consisted of a sharp drop. It was followed by a ninety-degree turn. I was looking at a deathtrap. It was waiting to engulf me. I said a quick prayer and pushed off. I did not know what lay ahead.

    I handled the steep drop with minimal effort. My luck ran out as I attempted to turn. I tried to maneuver around an unsuspecting skier. I lost control. I could not turn. I veered off the ski trail. Of course, I collided with the poor man. I also bent his pole. This seemed trivial to me as I swiftly headed over the side of the cliff. I was in mid-air for a few seconds. I rushed head-on into a gate.

    I lay there in the snow. I was stunned. I did not realize what had happened. Then, I heard my friends calling my name. I heard spectators asking if I were alive. I came back to reality. I had risked my life. I had been participating in something most people call a sport. Fortunately, only my pride was bruised. I will never again slide down mountains on little pieces of wood.

Chapter 24   Exercise A
Revising Sentence Fragments

The following passage contains fragments. On your own paper, rewrite the passage in complete sentences. Some of the fragments can be combined with independent clauses. For others, you will need to add a subject, a verb, or a new independent clause.

Today, more and more people are becoming interested in discovering their roots. Because of the popularity of a book by Alex Haley, called *Roots*. It tells the story of Haley's search for his ancestors. In Africa and other places. Before he wrote *Roots*, Haley worked on another book. *The Autobiography of Malcolm X*. After *Roots* was published. It became a bestseller. Then they made a movie for television based on it. Now, people of all backgrounds are interested in tracing their ancestry. A good book. A great man.

Chapter 24   Exercise B
Revising Sentence Fragments

The following passage contains fragments. On your own paper, rewrite the passage in complete sentences. Some of the fragments can be combined with independent clauses. For others, you will need to add a subject, a verb, or a new independent clause.

When we moved from an apartment to a house. We discovered that we had more belongings than we thought. So much stuff had to be packed. In the boxes. In suitcases. And even in large garbage bags. We rented a truck. From the local gas station. So we could avoid spending the extra money to hire a mover. We certainly put in a full day's work. That day. Although the process was long and hard. It was worth it.

Chapter 24   Exercise C
Revising Sentence Fragments

Use the conjunctions in parentheses to link the following short sentences or fragments. Rewrite and punctuate as necessary to generate a sentence that is smooth and correct.

Example: You should hurry. We are going to be late. (unless)

Unless you hurry, we are going to be late.

1. The program aired. The executives had debated whether to release it. (after)

_____

_____

2. The dining hall serves three meals a day. Students must eat during the serving hours. (however)

_____

_____

3. The western cowboy. The frontiersman. Blend truth with American mythology. (both, and)

_____

_____

Chapter 24   Exercise D
Revising Sentence Fragments

Use the conjunctions in parentheses to link the following short sentences or fragments. Rewrite and punctuate as necessary to generate a sentence that is smooth and correct.

Example: You should hurry. We are going to be late. (unless)

Unless you hurry, we are going to be late.

1. The officials did not like the thunder that shook the ground and lightning that brightened the sky. The soccer tournament was postponed until Saturday. (because)

    _____

    _____

2. Erica struck out eleven batters. She hit two doubles and drove in five runs. (not only, but also)

    _____

    _____

3. The administrators. The faculty. Correctly projected enrollment trends. (neither, nor)

    _____

    _____

Name _____ Date _____ Score _____

Chapter 25   Exercise A
Revising Comma Splices and Fused Sentences

Correct any run-ons or comma splices by inserting periods, commas, or semicolons as needed.

Example: The porch is sagging the window needs repair.

The porch is sagging; the window needs repair.

The porch is sagging. The window needs repair.

1. Linda is saving her money she wants to travel.

2. Brian could take Staci out for an enjoyable Mexican dinner and a movie he has enough money.

3. Clint and Ginger sold their television set now they do not miss it.

4. Don cleaned the apartment he cooked the dinner.

5. In graduate school, Louie once studied French and Spanish since then he has worked as a translator for the United Nations.

6. When the bridge closed, traffic was slowed for miles even leaving early did not help.

7. When you visit our campus for the interview, the most convenient parking lot is west of the building ask the attendant for directions to my office.

Chapter 25   Exercise B
Revising Comma Splices and Fused Sentences

In the space provided, mark a "C" for a complete sentence or "RO" for a run-on sentence. Draw a line between the independent clauses in run-ons.

1. _____ The president rose to speak, the audience listened.

2. _____ In the waiting room, one woman is writing a letter

    another reading a book about Chartres Cathedral.

3. _____ Brenda is actually the brain of the family's business,

    everyone should realize that by now.

4. _____ The group was small only twelve showed up.

5. _____ Answer, please, as soon as you can.

6. _____ The team has many talented players, Reece is the team's

    dependable shortstop.

7. _____ Ron built the deck, his craftsmanship is truly impressive.

8. _____ I am expecting a call has anyone telephoned?

9. _____ Johnny is respected for his attention to detail, each of his

    customers can be confident about the quality of work he

    provides.

10. _____ Last night I called you, I called several times.

Chapter 25   Exercise C
Revising Comma Splices and Fused Sentences

Correct these run-ons in each of the four ways you have learned.

1. Luke loves golf, he plays a round every sunny day.

a. _____

b. _____

c. _____

d. _____

2. Andy collects stamps he probably has that one.

a. _____

b. _____

c. _____

d. _____

3. Thomas enjoyed the sailboat he might buy a scooter.

a. _____

b. _____

c. _____

d. _____

Chapter 25   Exercise D
Revising Comma Splices and Fused Sentences

On your own paper, revise the following paragraph to change run-ons into complete and correct sentences.

Cats make great pets. You have to be affectionate to them. They are rather independent animals they do not always come when you call them. Many people prefer dogs, you can train them to come, or sit, or fetch a bone. With cats, on the other hand, you have to be willing to let them live their own lives if you attempt to train them you may become discouraged. If you put two cats in the same room, you are in for quite a treat. They chase each other, usually all in fun and when one catches the other the real show begins. Often they will cuddle and clean each other sometimes they will fight. The wise pet owner will know when to break up a fight and when to let it go since it is only play for the cats. They can be great company if you understand them.

Chapter 26   Exercise A
Revising Faulty Modification

In the space provided, write "C" if the sentence is correct as it stands. Write "DM" if it contains a dangling modifier.

1. _____ Shining brightly in the grass, Hattie stooped to pick up the silver coins that sparkled in the sunlight.

2. _____ While doing my homework, the supper burned.

3. _____ When you are ready, please drive me to school.

4. _____ Running to class, Arthur's digital clock pen was lost.

5. _____ The shirt is not only well made, but also attractive.

6. _____ Being antique cut-glass, she handled the bowl carefully as she examined its intricate design.

7. _____ Leslie saw three deer driving through the mountains.

8. _____ Having repaired the outside of the house, the inside needed a great deal of attention as well.

9. _____ To play golf, the eye must be kept on the ball.

10. _____ Eva sat for an hour, waiting for the lights to go out.

Chapter 26   Exercise B
Revising Faulty Modification

On your own paper, rewrite each of the following sentences to correct any faulty modification.

Example: Increasingly   concerned   about   the   environment, conservation has become a hot topic.

Because many people are increasingly concerned about the environment, conservation has become a hot topic. (dependent clause)

1. Although a small part of the world's population, proportionally more of the earth's nonrenewable natural resources are used up by people in developed countries.

2. As fossil fuels, minerals, metals, timber, and water are diminishing, replacement cannot happen because they were built up over billions of years.

3. Doubling every decade, time for change of world consumption of oil would seem short.

4. By flooding certain coastal areas, seawater evaporation extracts a few minerals, such as common salt, magnesium, and bromine.

5. Although polluting the atmosphere, one-half to one-third of the world's additional energy needs in the next twenty years will be satisfied by the use of coal, according to experts.

Chapter 26   Exercise C
Revising Faulty Modification

On your own paper, rewrite the following passage, correcting any sentences that contain misplaced modifiers.

These days, many people are trying health foods in all parts of the country. The "back to nature" movement has nearly affected everyone in one way or another. Producers of health foods use no preservatives in their products which they claim are bad for the system. Cereals such as granola a totally natural food are especially popular. People are also eating unstarched rice which is supposed to be good for the digestive system particularly. Ice cream even comes in new, natural flavors such as banana and coconut which is made with fresh bananas. Certainly health food companies are trying hard to attract customers interested in better nutrition.

Chapter 26   Exercise D
Revising Faulty Modification

On your own paper, rewrite the following passage, correcting any sentences that contain dangling modifiers.

On arriving in America, the sights and sounds amazed Pierre. Having traveled alone, so many people hurrying around and shouting came as a jolt to him. Coming from a small village in the south of France, so much commotion had never before been witnessed by the young traveler. And being only eight years old and a bit nervous, his luggage seemed to be his only companion. On this trip, his cousins in Philadelphia would be his hosts. After looking for them at the gate, and not being able to find them, an attendant took him to the information booth. Over the loudspeaker, Pierre's cousins were paged. To locate them, an announcement had to be made twice by the attendant. Then, running through the terminal, from the other end of the building, Pierre recognized his relatives. Feeling relieved, Pierre ran to them and escaped the crazy crowds of America.

Chapter 27   Exercise A
Revising Faulty Parallelism

Underline the word or phrase that maintains the parallel structure in each sentence.

1. At the party, Marjorie told us of her plans (to leave / and that she was leaving).

2. The more I think about the nuclear issue, the more one question (kept / keeps) entering my mind.

3. Whenever she has a spare moment, Jonna likes to read for entertainment and (enlightenment / to enlighten herself).

4. For months, Karen's friends have told her that her boyfriend is lazy, poor, and (that he lacked education / uneducated).

5. In Whitney's first letter, she told us that her dormitory room is twelve feet long and (ten feet in width / ten feet wide).

6. Having just finished reading his favorite author's most recent novel, Vernon claims that it is brilliant, informative and (humorous / has a lot of humor).

7. My father likes (the country / to live in the country), to walk in the fields, and to fish in the streams.

8. (You are either late / Either you are late) or I am early.

9. Leanne took up painting, writing, and (she taught / teaching) after she left the convent.

10. Dennis was surprised that Trish's favorite hobbies are swimming, playing the guitar, and (riding horseback / to ride horseback).

Chapter 27   Exercise B
Revising Faulty Parallelism

On your own paper, rewrite each of the following sentences in two ways, using effective and consistent parallelism in your revisions.

Example: Eat, drinking, and be merry.
          a. Eat, drink, and be merry.
          b. They love eating, drinking, and being merry.

1. Amy Rohling, one of the most talented people we know, is a painter, an actress, and who writes plays.

2. The camera takes clear pictures and that is easy to use.

3. Megan Nelson manages to hold a responsible position, earn an impressive salary, and she is writing a novel.

4. In the recording of popular music, the separate tasks of producing, arranging, and to engineer are often performed by one person who is called the producer.

5. When we are well rehearsed, when our timing is precise, and our singer is in good voice, we sound as good as any other band in the city.

6. On their first date, they were talking, ate, and drinking for hours after most others had left.

7. Laura refuses either to go by bus or by riding the subway.

8. Are marrying, child-rearing, and to shop all there is to life after graduate school?

9. At thirteen months, my grandson Michael exhibits remarkable agility of movement, he comprehends complex ideas, and aggressiveness of character.

Chapter 27   Exercise C
Revising Faulty Parallelism

Identify the parallel elements in these sentences by underlining parallel words and bracketing parallel phrases and clauses.

Example: Each morning, my roommate amazes me with her energy: she [wakes herself at four o'clock without an alarm], [jogs two miles], [cooks breakfast for both of us], [sends an e-mail to her mother], [calls her boyfriend], and [wears a smile all the while].

1.   Brian has developed a challenging training program: before breakfast, he jogs; after lunch, he bikes; and after supper, he swims.

2.   Beth and Erica agreed that it was one of the best films they'd seen in several months: its characters were believable, its camera work was intriguing, its soundtrack was spectacular, and its language was inoffensive.

3.   Angela worked all of her math problems, studied her Spanish assignment, read two history textbook chapters, and then wrote her composition.

4.   Before making the long journey to Panama City Beach for spring break, take these precautions: change the oil, fill the gas tank, check the tires' air pressure, and replace the windshield wipers.

5.   For a fishing trip that's certain to be memorable, my grandfather recommends the following preparations: pack your rod, reel, and tackle box; check the boat's motor; purchase gas and oil; and make plenty of peanut butter and jelly sandwiches.

Chapter 27   Exercise D
Revising Faulty Parallelism

On your own paper, revise the following paragraphs, using parallelism and balance whenever possible to highlight corresponding elements and using repetition of key words and phrases to add emphasis. (To achieve repetition, you must change some synonyms.) You may combine sentences, and you may add, delete, or reorder words.

For hundreds and thousands of years, the Nile Valley experienced an annual flood. The yearly floodwaters of the Nile carried soil particles from upstream. The soil particles were deposited throughout the flood plain. The silt deposited by the yearly flood renewed the fertility of the Egyptian fields. This yearly event might be interpreted as a natural disaster. Rather than being a natural disaster, the annual flood permitted the rise of one of the richest of ancient civilizations. It was also one of the most advanced ancient civilizations. The annual flood enabled the people to grow enough food to support a large population. There was enough food for people for other activities. Some of these activities included building, scholarship, and art.

During the past century, the Aswan High Dam was constructed. There have been enormous changes in the Nile Valley. The Aswan High Dam is designed to retain an entire annual flow of the Nile. The Aswan High Dam also provides power to make cheap fertilizers. These fertilizers are needed by the intensively cultivated farms that are no longer covered by silty Nile water, which had previously renewed soil fertility. The Aswan High Dam has ended the annual flooding of the Nile Valley. The Nile used to bring nutritious silt to the region. The nutritious silt was once cherished for its nutrients. Many people now consider the silt a nuisance. The silt is considered a nuisance because it fills up irrigation canals.

Chapter 28   Exercise A
Revising Awkward or Confusing Sentences

Review the following sentences for incorrect shifts in tense, person, number, voice, and mood. Underline the mismatched words.

Example: When I <u>tell</u> him that he is cute, he <u>grinned</u>.

1. I close the door because I needed to be left alone.

2. Bill wants to study medicine, but he dreaded the thought of four more years in school.

3. On our trip to Europe last summer, we stay at the best hotels, and we paid the highest prices.

4. Michael washed the dishes and then he begins to bake the cookies.

5. Ed runs well over one hundred miles each week and hoped to qualify for the Olympics.

6. When Reece entered the room, he adjusts the antenna and then changed the channel.

7. Anyone can learn French if they will only try.

8. After one is under water for ten minutes, they will have difficulty breathing.

9. If you adhere strictly to a vegetarian diet, one cannot eat steak, chicken, fish, or pork.

10. In her novel, Jane Austen creates a society that acts according to their characters' social expectations.

Chapter 28   Exercise B
Revising Awkward or Confusing Sentences

On your own paper, rewrite each of the following sentences in two ways to correct the shifts in tense, person, number, voice, and mood.

Example: When I <u>tell</u> him that he is cute, he <u>grinned</u>.
             When I tell him that he is cute, he grins.
             When I told him that he is cute, he grinned.

1. I close the door because I needed to be left alone.

2. Bill wants to study medicine, but he dreaded the thought of four more years in school.

3. On our trip to Europe, we stay at the best hotels, and we paid the highest prices.

4. Michael washed the dishes and then he begins to bake the cookies.

5. Ed runs well over one hundred miles each week and hoped to qualify for the Olympics.

Chapter 28   Exercise C
Revising Awkward or Confusing Sentences

On your own paper, rewrite each of the following sentences in two ways to correct the shifts in tense, person, number, voice, and mood.

Example: When I <u>tell</u> him that he is cute, he <u>grinned</u>.
When I tell him that he is cute, he grins.
When I told him that he is cute, he grinned.

1. When Reece entered the room, he adjusts the antenna and then changed the channel.

2. Anyone can learn French if they will only try.

3. After one is under water for ten minutes, they will have difficulty breathing.

4. If you adhere strictly to a vegetarian diet, one cannot eat steak, chicken, fish, or pork.

5. In her novel, Jane Austen creates a society that acts according to their characters' social expectations.

Chapter 28   Exercise D
Revising Awkward or Confusing Sentences

On your own paper, rewrite the following passages to eliminate any incorrect shifts in tense, number, person, voice, or mood.

I work in a bank, and when you have that type of job, you have to be willing to wake up at a very early hour. Each morning, I drive to work, park my car, and walked a block to work. I get a lunch break every day at noon, and they love to eat at the delicatessen around the corner. I worked at the bank for over a year, and decided that I had had enough. After looking around for a new job, I found one where you had to be at work at 6:00 a.m. This job was in a restaurant where you had to stand up all day, and after six months, I decided to go back to the bank. The manager was very nice to me and says, "You can have your old job back if one promises to stay at least two years." I take the job, and I enjoyed an extra hour of sleep every morning.

Review Exercise A for Part 4, Chapters 24–28
Solving Common Sentence Problems

Label the type of problem found in each of the following entries. For your labels, select from the following list:

comma splice   fused sentence
dangling modifier   agreement error
sentence fragment

1. On the Philmont trek, each scout packed his own water supply, compass, and rain gear. Also a share of the troop's tents and cooking equipment.

   _____

2. Thomas loaded the bottles and cans into his new Porsche, which he planned to leave at the recycling center.

   _____

3. Luke has missed work for seven consecutive days, he's concerned that his job is in jeopardy.

   _____

4. Andy bunted safely three times in yesterday's game he also stole home to score the winning run.

   _____

(This exercise continues on the next page.)

5. Beth explained, speaking directly to her father, how well she had run her race at the track meet.

_____

6. History can be exciting and engaging too often it is presented in a boring manner.

_____

7. Our family was surprised as we drove through Badlands National Park, the bleak landscape was oppressive.

_____

8. One of my favorite cities in the world is Edinburgh. London, Paris, and Rome, too.

_____

9. Margaret watched the colorful sailboats taking an afternoon jog along the shore.

_____

Review Exercise B for Part 4, Chapters 24–28
Solving Common Sentence Problems

On your own paper, rewrite the following student draft to eliminate misplaced and dangling modifiers, faulty parallelism, shifts, mixed constructions, and faulty predication. Change and rearrange sentences as necessary.

Making Waffles

After a long night's sleep, how would you like to sit down to a cup of hot coffee and golden brown waffles for breakfast? You would probably like them with warm strawberries and a scoop of fresh, whipped cream, or you prefer the traditional butter and maple syrup. Waffles are, in any case, an excellent breakfast dish, and there are many ways to serve them, for they are easy to prepare. Basically, making waffles involves three steps: preparing the batter, cooking the waffle, and you have to decide how to top it.

First, before mixing the batter is where to preheat the waffle iron. Most irons have to be plugged in, and usually it took from ten to fifteen minutes to heat up. I have found that medium is usually the best setting, but which setting works best for you will have to be decided.

The batter is a relatively simple task. First, combine the following in a large mixing bowl: one cup of cake flour, two tablespoons of sugar, two teaspoons of baking powder, and finally add one-fourth teaspoon of salt.

Next, add one cup of milk and one tablespoon of vegetable oil to the dry ingredients. Oil is an important step; otherwise, the waffles will be stuck to the iron. If you don't have any vegetable oil, one tablespoon of melted butter or margarine can be used. Use a medium-sized spoon to stir the batter until it forms without any lumps in it a smooth mixture.

(This exercise continues on the next page.)

Review Exercise B for Part 4, Chapters 24–28
Solving Common Sentence Problems (continued)

After thoroughly stirring the batter, making sure that there aren't any lumps in it, two eggs should be cracked into a small bowl. Take care not to break the yolks, and there shouldn't be any pieces of shell in the bowl.

Next, separate the yolks with a small spoon, and store them, since they will not be added to the batter, in an appropriate container. Using a small fork to beat the egg whites will become frothy. Then, combine the egg whites with the batter, mixing them in completely. Preparing the egg whites in this manner, it seems like a waste of time when you could just toss them into the batter. But this way, the waffles turn out with a light texture on the inside and fluffy too.

By this time, the preheating of the waffle iron is probably finished. Some batter should be put in the waffle iron, filling all of the ridges of the iron's bottom side, using a mixing spoon. Now, use a low, medium, or high setting to cook the waffle to your desired preference, golden brown, or for some, burned. These instructions will produce four medium-sized waffles.

Finally, the hardest part of preparing waffles is deciding what topping to use. Whatever topping you decide to use—fruit and cream, butter and syrup, or even ice cream—waffles are always a special, as well as a splendid addition to anyone's breakfast menu treat. Try them sometime.

Chapter 29   Exercise A
Choosing Words

In the space below, write a paragraph in which you encourage a friend to read a book or see a movie that you have recently enjoyed. Underline the words that you include specifically to convey your favorable opinion to your friend.

_____

_____

_____

_____

_____

_____

_____

_____

_____

_____

Chapter 29   Exercise B
Choosing Words

In the space below, write a paragraph in which you attempt to persuade Aunt Sally to permit you to borrow her 1962 pickup truck for your move to a new apartment. Remember that Aunt Sally has long been reluctant to let anyone drive the truck because it was the pride and joy of Uncle Ralph. Underline the words that you include specifically to display your respectful attitude toward your aunt, your late uncle, and his precious truck.

_____

_____

_____

_____

_____

_____

_____

_____

_____

Chapter 29   Exercise C
Choosing Words

In the space below, write a paragraph in which you include at least four of the commonly used figures of speech mentioned on pages 471–72 of *The Holt Handbook*. In the margin adjacent to each figure of speech, write a label to identify your intentions.

_____

_____

_____

_____

_____

_____

_____

_____

_____

_____

Chapter 29   Exercise D
Choosing Words

In the space below, rewrite the paragraph that you wrote for Exercise C, and eliminate the figures of speech that you intentionally included.

_____

_____

_____

_____

_____

_____

_____

_____

_____

_____

_____

Name _____ Date _____ Score _____

Chapter 30   Exercise A
Using a Dictionary

Use a college dictionary to answer the following questions about grammatical form.

1. What are the principal parts of the following verbs:

drink _____

deify _____

carol _____

draw _____

ring _____

2. Some of the nouns in the following list can be used as verbs. Underline those that can be used as verbs.

   canter, council, command, lord, minister, mother

3. What are the plural forms of these nouns?

silo _____

sheep _____

seed _____

scissors _____

genetics _____

alchemy _____

Chapter 30   Exercise B
Using a Dictionary

Use a college dictionary to answer the following questions about grammatical form.

1. What are the comparative and superlative forms of the following adverbs and adjectives?

	comparative	superlative
fast	_____	_____
airy	_____	_____
mere	_____	_____
homey	_____	_____
unlucky	_____	_____

2. Are the following verbs transitive, intransitive, or both?

become _____

elect _____

find _____

give _____

Chapter 30   Exercise C
Using a Dictionary

Consult a dictionary to help you divide each of these words into syllables. Then indicate with a hyphen where you would divide each word at the end of a line.

Example:

underground   un • der • ground   under-ground

1. amazing _____

2. bookkeeper _____

3. calliope _____

4. longitude _____

5. markedly _____

6. martyr _____

7. side-splitting _____

8. thorough _____

9. transcendentalism _____

10. unlikely _____

Chapter 30   Exercise D
Using a Dictionary

To test the research capability of your dictionary, use it to answer the following questions.

1. In what year did Anwar el-Sadat win the Nobel Peace Prize?

    _____

2. After whom was the Ferris wheel named?

    _____

3. What is the atomic weight of sulfur? _____

4. What is the full name of the French playwright known as Molière?

    _____

5. Define *surrealism*?

    _____

    _____

Chapter 31   Exercise A
Improving Spelling

Write "C" if the word is correctly spelled. If it is misspelled, write it correctly in the space provided.

1. Wendsday   _____

2. arrangment   _____

3. couragously   _____

4. simular   _____

5. applyed   _____

6. potatos   _____

7. admitance   _____

8. hinderence   _____

9. athelete   _____

10. kindergarden   _____

11. exaduration   _____

12. suprize   _____

13. enterance   _____

14. eventhough   _____

Chapter 31   Exercise B
Improving Spelling

Underline the correctly spelled word in the parentheses.

1. Jonna will not (except / accept) his present.

2. Vince's hard work (affected / effected) his grades.

3. Raleigh is the (capital / capitol) city of North Carolina.

4. Don't just (lay / lie) there; hop up and answer the phone.

5. To Jim's surprise, no one was (their / there).

6. We allow no (acception / exception) to this rule.

7. Did you (lose / loose) your wallet?

8. Don't forget to renew your driver's (license / lisense).

9. (Driveing / Driving) without one is a crime.

10. If you have renewed it (already / allready), don't worry.

11. Don't drive without it in your (posession / possession).

12. Some (friendly / freindly) officer might ask to see it.

Name _____ Date _____ Score _____

Review Exercise A for Part 5, Chapters 29–31
Using Words Effectively

1. You've just returned from your month-long trip to the location of your choice. As a graduation gift, your wealthy aunt let you select your destination—anywhere in the world—and paid all of your expenses. In the space below, use diction appropriate for your friends to write a one-paragraph description of your vacation.

_____

_____

_____

_____

_____

_____

_____

_____

_____

_____

(This exercise continues on the next page.)

2. In the space below, write another one-paragraph description of your
    vacation; in this account, however, use diction appropriate for your
    wealthy aunt, who wants to hear the details. Remember that Aunt
    Eda is the former president of the local chapter of the Daughters of
    the American Revolution. By the way, when you're speaking with
    your aunt, two of her closest friends will be present in your aunt's
    parlor.

_____

_____

_____

_____

_____

_____

_____

_____

_____

Review Exercise B for Part 5, Chapters 29–31
Using Words Effectively

On your own paper, revise the following student draft for appropriateness, accuracy, and freshness. Where appropriate, include figurative language. Change words and rewrite sentences as necessary.

Pilot Mountain

My favorite place is a unique mountain surrounded by trees. Its beauty is better than all the modernization of man below it. It has a unique rock formation. Nowhere on this earth can you find another such creation that could even compare.

_____

_____

_____

_____

_____

_____

_____

_____

_____

_____

(This exercise continues on the next page.)

Review Exercise B for Part 5, Chapters 29–31 (continued)
Using Words Effectively

The Little Pinnacle is where you want to look at the knob. Through all the mountain's original symmetry, the Little Pinnacle still remains the most breath-taking point. To reach this point, one must climb a long path full of lots of obstacles. After the hike one can rest on a rock and marvel at the wonders of nature.

_____

_____

_____

_____

_____

The most famous point on the mountain is the Knob. Looking from the Little Pinnacle, one can see lots of tall, straight trees growing on top of the Knob. The walls of the Knob are stone. No plants grow there. It all looks pretty funny. You can see the Knob from lots of other places in the area, but this view is still the best.

_____

_____

_____

_____

_____

Chapter 32   Exercise A
Parts of Speech: Nouns

Underline the nouns in the following sentences.

Example: Most <u>students</u> go to the weekly <u>dances</u>.

1. In spite of the terrible downpour, 107,000 fans attended the game and stayed until the final buzzer.
2. At the lake last summer, we fished each morning, swam each afternoon, and hiked each evening.
3. The campus bookstore will be open late on Tuesday night, but it will close early on Friday afternoon.
4. The University of North Carolina, located in the town of Chapel Hill, has buildings that date back to colonial days.
5. The fencing team is a small group of dedicated athletes.
6. The newspaper comes out every week and is noted for its lively articles and controversial columns.
7. The crew of the lunar module performed the scheduled tasks and experiments before returning to base.
8. Math exams can be especially challenging for students whose majors are in the humanities.
9. Neil Armstrong was the first person to walk on the moon.
10. Chicken with mashed potatoes is my favorite meal.

Chapter 32   Exercise B
Parts of Speech: Pronouns

Underline the correct pronoun in each sentence.

Example: Amy and (<u>she</u> / her) have excellent study habits.

1. They pushed Adam and (I / me) down the hill.

2. The sisters raced to (her / their) treehouse.

3. The Risers and (we / us) plan to camp this weekend.

4. The team's trophy is for (its / its) outstanding sportsmanship.

5. Wanda and (I / me) will give our reports today.

6. (Who / Whom) was looking for me this morning?

7. (Who / Whom) did you meet at the airport?

8. To (who / whom) did you address the letter?

9. The new employees, Beth and (I / me), began the training program immediately.

10. The company's training program was designed for the new employees, Beth and (I / me).

11. Many of (we / us) students take classes and hold jobs.

12. (Him / He) and Margaret made a detailed map of the area.

13. Between you and (I / me), the new boss is great.

14. Jim knows more about zoology than (she / her).

15. Sarah received the package from (I / me) on time.

Chapter 32   Exercise C
Parts of Speech: Pronouns

Underline the correct pronoun in each sentence.

1. They suspected that the prankster was (he / him).

2. I would not want to be (she / her).

3. Neither the general nor the soldier lost (his / their) life.

4. All of us have to do (her / our) jobs in this organization.

5. I left my coat with Fay and (they / them).

6. (We / Us) athletes all went out for the team.

7. My sister and (they / them) are good friends.

8. Who sent this package to (me / myself)?

9. All that confusion was caused by (him / himself).

10. I wish I were as easygoing as (they / themselves).

11. (He and I / Him and me) prefer to listen to classical music.

12. Neither Trish nor Kathy missed (her / their) class.

13. Eight of the plants produced (its / their) flowers as expected.

14. (Who / Whom) is the candidate of your choice?

15. For (who / whom) will you cast your vote?

Chapter 32   Exercise D
Parts of Speech: Verbs

In the space provided, write "C" if the example has a complete verb or
"I" if it has an incomplete verb.

1. _____ Brian and Beth visited Yosemite National Park.

2. _____ All members of the Beta Club to attend the baseball game.

3. _____ Scouts with flashlights served as guides along the path.

4. _____ What the surgeon told the class of interns.

5. _____ My computer has crashed only once this week.

6. _____ Crashed or froze ten times last week.

7. _____ Most students prefer to purchase used textbooks.

8. _____ Everybody to hurry for shelter.

9. _____ With friends they enjoying the snow.

10. _____ Mike and Diane making snowballs.

11. _____ The wind blowing and chilling.

12. _____ A blizzard might have been coming.

13. _____ Errands to the bank, the post office, and the bakery.

14. _____ Why are all research papers due just before Thanksgiving?

15. _____ The rain in Spain mainly on the plain.

Chapter 32   Exercise E
Parts of Speech: Verbs

Complete each sentence by underlining the appropriate form of the verb in parentheses.

Example: The fisherman (<u>caught</u> / was caught by) the trout.

1. The attorney (reviewed / was reviewed by) the contracts.

2. The dog (combed / was combed by) its trainer.

3. The professor (graded / was graded by) the essays.

4. The church bell (rang / was rung by) the elderly caretaker.

5. The hungry loggers (ate / were eaten by) the pancakes.

6. The pancakes (ate / were eaten by) the hungry loggers.

7. The prize cucumber (grew / was grown by) Cathy Cowart.

8. Amanda (answered / was answered by) every question in the review section at the end of the chapter.

9. Each e-mail submission to the contest (answers / is answered by) the computer, which sends an acknowledgement by return e-mail.

10. When a caller leaves a message, it (records / is recorded by) the answering machine.

11. Occasionally the tape (skips / is skipped by) a message.

12. The cat (has untangled / has been untangled by) the ball of twine.

Chapter 32   Exercise F
Parts of Speech: Adjectives

Underline the correct adjective in each sentence.

1. Sarah's hair is naturally (curled / curly).

2. In two pages, write (a / an) history of American film.

3. Brenda looks (tired / tiredly).

4. Reece wears only (sloppy / sloppily) clothes.

5. What an (unsightly / unsighted) mess!

6. Ronnie waited for this (luckily / lucky) break.

7. Casey combed her (gold / golden) hair.

8. The strawberry jam is too (sweet / sweetly).

9. Laura stopped at (their / theirs) apartment yesterday.

10. (Each / Both) sheep are ready for shearing.

11. (Each / Both) sheep has its own pedigree.

12. (This / These) crew will report for duty tomorrow.

13. (This / These) crew members are on vacation.

14. The movie had one (tense / tenser) moment after another.

15. Negotiators avoided (a / an) union strike.

Chapter 32   Exercise G
Parts of Speech: Adjectives

Underline the adjectives in the following sentences.

1. The staff worked best with a definite deadline.

2. Jessie grabbed her old boots and ran hurriedly.

3. The six dogs ran ahead, playfully romping in the high grass.

4. The trip is rather long, but we usually arrive in two days.

5. We anxiously awaited Mother's call to eat the delicious meal that she had meticulously placed on a beautifully decorated table.

6. Diane carelessly left her blue backpack in the classroom.

7. Very soon the cold water began dripping loudly on the parquet floor in the vacant room.

8. Joel may be quite tall, but he has never played basketball.

9. From their dazed appearance, we concluded that each exhausted hiker was ready for a warm bath, a bowl of hot soup, and a long rest in a cozy bed.

10. In the final competition, the group of four students worked amazingly well together as they addressed each perplexing task that the committee presented.

Chapter 32   Exercise H
Parts of Speech: Adverbs

Underline the correct adverb in each sentence.

1. To close the window, turn the crank (gentle / gently).

2. Raise the garage door as (careful / carefully) as possible.

3. Even in the worst weather, Trish is (seldom / seldomly) late.

4. Weeks of practice paid off when the play was executed (perfect / perfectly) and Jamie's team won the game in the final seconds.

5. Don fought (manly / manfully) for his rights.

6. Fay could (usual / usually) run quickly.

7. Erica (rare / rarely) displays anger on the field.

8. Everyone thought (high / highly) of Coach Cowart.

9. Loose gravel convinced them to ride (slow / slowly) on their bikes.

10. In spite of the muddy track, the horse raced (fast / fastly).

11. I enjoy watching the camels running (graceful / gracefully).

12. The children ran (wild / wildly) across the playground.

13. Cathy visited her mother (often / oftenly).

14. The bell rang (more loudly / most loudly) than ever.

15. The green team finished (last / lastly).

Chapter 32   Exercise I
Parts of Speech: Adverbs

Underline the adverbs in the following sentences.

1. The staff worked best with a definite deadline.

2. Jessie grabbed her old boots and ran hurriedly.

3. Julie actually knew she would do well on the exam.

4. The dog's heart beat loudly as he panted rapidly.

5. Camille's extremely regal appearance surprised her friends.

6. We sometimes review customer accounts randomly.

7. The six dogs ran ahead, playfully romping in the high grass.

8. Stomach pains are most often caused by overeating.

9. They danced gracefully despite the band's mistakes.

10. The trip is rather long, but we usually arrive in two days.

11. We anxiously awaited Mother's call to eat the delicious meal that

    she had meticulously placed on a beautifully decorated table.

12. Diane carelessly left her blue backpack in the classroom.

13. Very soon the cold water began dripping loudly on the parquet

    floor in the vacant room.

14. Joel may be quite tall, but he has never played basketball.

15. Claire is unlikely to be home now; try again tomorrow.

Chapter 32   Exercise J
Parts of Speech: Prepositions

For each sentence, underline the most logical of the prepositions in parentheses.

1. The balloon descended (above / around / to) the ground.

2. The ten children got along well (in spite of / by way of / between) their age differences.

3. As the children watched helplessly, the ball rolled (with / across / on account of) the concrete driveway.

4. To everyone's amazement, the magician waved his wand and then lofted the rabbit (beyond / in back of / above) his head.

5. (After / Before / Between) the storm left the area, the sky darkened, thunder rumbled, and the rain came down in buckets.

6. (Among / Between / In spite of) you and me, I think this will be an action-packed spring break.

7. At night during the summer months, the city lights cast a spooky glow (within / up to / behind) the dark hill.

8. To the dismay of the judge, the news spread rapidly (between / among / through) the jury members.

9. The monster growled and crept slowly (to / toward / regarding) the cowering heroine.

10. In our neighborhood, the Sunday newspaper always arrives (until / during / before) 8:15 A.M.

Chapter 32   Exercise K
Parts of Speech: Prepositions

Underline the prepositions in the following sentences.

1. At the beginning of the term, the bookstore is not an enjoyable place to visit because it is too crowded.

2. Despite being excited about new courses, students are needlessly exhausted by the lines at the bookstore.

3. All the books are arranged under the names of the departments, so I had to make several stops to find mine.

4. When other students blocked the aisles, I had to push by to get to the right place to find my books.

5. The books for my English course were on the top shelf.

6. To get them, I had to climb up on a ladder that was shaking because of the jostling crowd.

7. My fear of heights, however, was less than my fear of being trampled when I found my math books on the bottom shelf, behind those for calculus.

8. After my books were gathered up, I saw that the lines for the cashiers wound behind the sweatshirts and in front of the dictionaries.

9. I stood in line for an hour, thumbing through my books and talking with other students during the wait.

10. At last I had my books and was ready to practice my weight lifting on the long walk back to my room.

11. My mom thinks I'm too much of a complainer, but what does she know about life at college?

Chapter 32   Exercise L
Parts of Speech: Prepositions

Complete the sentences below by filling in the most logical prepositions from the following list.

against   at   during   in   into
of   on   under   with

Example: The Gunpowder Plot occurred _on_____
            November 5, 1605.

1. _____ that time of religious strife, King James I
   ruled England, a Protestant country.
2. _____ November 5, he was to open Parliament
   with a formal ceremony.
3. The plan of the Catholic conspirators was to blow up Parliament
   _____ that time.
4. Then they expected their fellow English Catholics to rise up
   _____ the Protestant government that suppressed
   their religion.
5. To carry out their plot, the conspirators had rented a cellar
   _____ Westminster, where the House of Lords
   met.
6. There they had stored thirty-six kegs of gunpowder, covered
   _____ firewood and coal.
7. Some members _____ the House of Lords
   received warning letters, urging them not to attend.
8. The secret cellar was discovered, and one conspirator, Guy
   Fawkes, was arrested when he came _____ the cellar.
9. _____ England, November 5 is still called Guy
   Fawkes Day.
10. _____ that day, fireworks and bonfires
    commemorate the discovery of the plot.

Chapter 32   Exercise M
Parts of Speech: Conjunctions

Underline the conjunctions in the following sentences.

Example: They were so hungry that they ate <u>not</u> <u>only</u>
            the eggs and sausage <u>but</u> <u>also</u> the doughnuts
            <u>and</u> coffeecake.

1. Both Carol and Doug enjoy the circus clowns.

2. Either Don will buy the clock, or he will pass up a great offer.

3. Staci and Linda had to wait in the hall until the doors opened.

4. Each member of the soccer team played her best game of the
    season; consequently, none of them should have any regrets.

5. Normally the course has a prerequisite; nevertheless, the professor
    may admit a student without it.

6. Unless Beth leaves now, she will miss the return flight.

7. The lectures are twice a week; in addition, students must attend
    weekly labs and discussion groups.

8. Erica selected the college because it has a fine reputation.

9. Neither her mother nor her father expected her to call.

10. Morning came, yet the sky remained gray.

11. Call the fire department or the ambulance squad.

12. The police officer assured me that the burglar alarm would continue
    to ring unless someone turns it off.

Name _____ Date _____ Score _____

Chapter 32   Exercise N
Parts of Speech: Conjunctions

Underline the correct conjunction in each sentence.

Example: She eats constantly (and / <u>but</u>) remains thin.

1. (Since / Because) the school was founded, it has offered courses in theology and ethics.

2. The department of religion (and / but) philosophy offers both courses each semester.

3. (While / Once) you wait for your interview, you might want to review the job requirements.

4. I had to take the 8 a.m. section (because / although) that was the only vacant slot in my schedule.

5. She knew when the paper was due; (consequently / nevertheless), she handed it in a week late.

6. He wanted to take a course in nearly every department; (moreover / for example), he thought everyone should read Shakespeare, study philosophy, and review American history.

7. Look in the dining hall (or / but) in the lounge.

8. Neither the regular fire drills (nor / but also) the occasional false alarms had prepared the students for the trauma of the real fire that struck their dorm that stormy winter night.

9. The crocuses were blooming (although / before) snow still covered the ground.

10. The baby refuses to eat (lest / unless) her grandmother feeds her.

Chapter 32   Exercise O
Parts of Speech: Conjunctions

Use the conjunctions in parentheses to link the following short
sentences or fragments. Rewrite and punctuate as necessary to generate a
sentence that is smooth and correct.

Example: You should hurry. We are going to be late. (unless)
            Unless you hurry, we are going to be late.

1. The program aired. The executives had debated whether to release
    it. (before)

    _____

2. The dining hall serves three meals a day. Students must eat during
    the serving hours. (however)

    _____

    _____

3. The neighbors' dog. The neighbors' goat. Make so much noise
    that they provide security against intruders. (both, and)

    _____

4. The administrators. The faculty. Correctly projected enrollment
    trends. (neither, nor)

    _____

Chapter 32   Exercise P
Parts of Speech: Interjections

Underline the interjections in the following sentences.

1. Wow! Can you imagine how excited Beth was?

2. From the examination room, I heard someone yell, "Ouch!"

    There's no way I'm staying here. I'll see you at home.

3. When I ask Grandma, she always says, "Oh, you're just like your

    father when he was your age."

4. When the mouse ran through the garage, Aunt Alice shouted,

    "Heavens!" and then grabbed the broom.

Chapter 33   Exercise A
Nouns and Pronouns

Underline the nouns and pronouns that are examples of the case specified in parentheses for each sentence.

Example: (nominative or subjective) The <u>cat</u> ate the canary.

1. (nominative or subjective) The doctor is the speaker who will appear first.

2. (possessive) Our cat lay on my mother's bed and licked the boy's chewing gum from its paw.

3. (objective) Whom did you invite to the party?

4. (nominative or subjective) We will go there tomorrow.

5. (possessive) The governor's speech astounded many members of his audience.

6. (objective) Give it to them or they'll complain to me.

7. (nominative or subjective) She is as serious as he.

8. (possessive) The police asked whose purse was missing.

9. (nominative or subjective) The brothers, Allen and Gene, live in different states.

10. (possessive) Ethan's swimming at noon is a daily ritual.

11. (objective) I sat behind him and her.

12. (possessive) His coat is in their hall closet.

13. (possessive) Dr. Edmundson's lectures are packed with interesting stories.

14. (nominative or subjective) They can't walk far at this hour and in this weather.

Chapter 33   Exercise B
Nouns and Pronouns

In the space provided write "C" if the sentence is correct as it stands or "X" if it contains an error in possessive form. Circle and correct the incorrect form.

1. _____ In this group of students, their the innovators.

2. _____ They're opinion is considered important here.

3. _____ Whose the group that presented the asteroid project that

won first place in the contest?

4. _____ Who's turn is it to feed the piranha?

5. _____ The womens' softball team has been undefeated in the last

four tournaments in which it has competed.

Chapter 33   Exercise C
Nouns and Pronouns

Underline the correct pronoun in each sentence.

1. The cat likes both Liz and (her / she).

2. Two were chosen, Jamie and (he / him), for the team.

3. Having appointed Casey as their representative, every member of the club was convinced that (her / she) would represent them well.

4. (She / Her) and Allison played soccer for the same team.

5. It must be (he / his) car in the driveway.

6. The librarian checked out the videos to (me / I).

7. Royce hates broccoli; it must be (you / yours).

8. We wanted to go shopping with Nancy and (she / her).

9. I gave (he / him) the dog when we moved out of town.

10. Amy counts (they / them) among her best friends.

11. Don asked Amanda and (I / me) for our opinions.

12. The club decided to revise (its / their) schedule.

13. The band's producer and (she / her) have arrived.

14. Fortunately, it was (we / us) who heard the news.

15. The dean approved of (us / our) working together.

Chapter 33   Exercise D
Nouns and Pronouns

Write a sentence using each of the following word pairs.

Example: computer   its

When the computer crashed for the seventh time this
afternoon, I simply pulled its plug and took a nap.

they   theirs

_____

_____

firefighter   who

_____

_____

technician   she

_____

_____

bicycles   their

_____

_____

Chapter 33   Exercise E
Nouns and Pronouns

On your own paper, rewrite the following sentences, eliminating any faulty pronoun references.

1. We could not find a parking space, which was why we were late for the surprise party.

2. Madeline told Savannah that her acceptance speech was one of the best presented following the elections.

3. When Julianna put the vase on the mantle, it fell down.

4. Backpacking is Allen's favorite outdoor activity. That is why he spends most weekends in the mountains.

5. When Beth sings that song, it drives her brother crazy.

6. Bev decided not to take the free ride on a hang glider, which allowed Gene to stop worrying.

7. Michael told Karie that his brother had won first place in the contest for the most original Halloween costume.

8. Ethan collects stamps, which provides him with a hobby that he shares with his grandfather.

9. The vocal group of residents convinced the company's board of directors not to build a factory near the town, which gave them a feeling of success.

Chapter 33   Exercise F
Nouns and Pronouns

Underline the correct word in the parentheses.

1. The members of the singing ensemble agreed to wear (their /
    they're / there) yellow toboggans for tonight's winter concert.

2. (Who's / Whose) team will win the tournament?

3. Who wrote "Beauty is (its / it's) own excuse for being"?

4. (Its / It's) puzzling that Chris hasn't been seen for several days.

5. Most of your classmates confuse you and (your / you're) twin.

6. Vince provided a model for (their / they're / there) design.

7. (Who's / Whose) sitting in that chair by the window?

8. The (governors / governor's) office has been evacuated.

9. (Womens / Women's / Womens') hats were far more popular in
    my grandmother's era.

10. Did you make a good grade on (your / you're) test?

Chapter 34   Exercise A
Verbs

Underline the correct verb in each sentence.

1. Although some floats (was / were) ruined by the downpour, the parade began as scheduled.

2. Everybody on the van (want / wants) an order of onion rings and a chocolate milk shake.

3. Although the variety of student backgrounds (make / makes) the class extremely challenging to manage, Mr. Hansard appreciates the stimulating and rewarding class.

4. Each member of the troop realizes that this Eagle Service Project (provide / provides) valuable service to the community.

5. Each member of the committee (has / have) been contacted by the secretary about the next meeting.

6. Many members of the board of directors (think / thinks) that the stock offering will be an immense success.

7. The competition is so keen that neither contestant (wants / want) to give her opponent an advantage.

8. To prepare for the competition, Brian and Joanna (ride / rides) their bicycles several miles each day.

9. Every camper (enjoy / enjoys) "water balloon madness," which is the final activity on the first day of camp.

10. Each of the scholars on this school's Science Olympiad team (devote / devotes) a minimum of ten hours of preparation each week by surfing the Internet for helpful sites.

Chapter 34   Exercise B
Verbs

Underline the complete verb of each sentence.

1. Michelle and Mary moved to Hawaii three years ago.

2. Many people knit and sew their own cardigans.

3. There were shadows flickering in the firelight.

4. These candles could light the entire room.

5. Often, though, the candles sputter, flicker, and drip.

6. Jonathan Swift wrote *Gulliver's Travels*.

7. What else did he write?

8. Andrew and Jacob will be responsible for this project.

9. Hot peppers should be used sparingly.

10. What will the future bring?

11. Brian and Beth visited Yosemite National Park.

12. Every Beta Club member hopes to attend the baseball game.

13. Scouts could have served as guides along the path.

14. My computer has crashed only once this week.

15. Most students would prefer to purchase used textbooks.

16. The prowler has been seen in many areas of the neighborhood.

Chapter 34   Exercise C
Verbs

Underline the most logical verb form in each sentence.

1. Marjorie quietly opened the door, pushed her head inside, and (had looked / looked / will look) around the room.

2. If Madeline (would have studied / studies / had studied), she would have passed the chemistry semester exam.

3. As you and Julianna must certainly know, for the past two hours I (am / was / have been) busy studying.

4. With several of his neighbors and fraternity brothers, Dwight (celebrate / celebrated / had celebrated) his birthday last night.

5. Before I head for class each morning, I eat breakfast, ride my bicycle, and (do / does / am doing) my exercises.

6. We will try harder, and we (do / did / will do) a much better job next time—if we get the opportunity.

7. The house (is built / was builded / was built) during the terrible heat wave last July and August.

8. Savannah tossed the ball, and I (catch / catches / caught) it.

9. Only after he had arrived home from the store did Ethan realize that he (forgot / had forgotten / forgets) to buy bread, milk, eggs, yogurt, and a can of tuna fish.

10. After the performers had taken their final curtain call, the lights in the theater (dim / dimmed / had dimmed).

Chapter 34   Exercise D
Verbs

Complete each sentence by filling in the correct form of the verb in parentheses.

Example: We won the homecoming game last year,
              but we _____*lost*_____ (lose) it this year.

1. Mr. Hansard _____ (escort) a group of students

    to France last year, and he intends _____

    (take) another group to Spain next year. But Brian and Beth

    _____ (wait) one more year for his trip to

    Scotland and England.

2. After I had completed my lab report, I _____ (begin)

    to plan my English essay.

3. Elizabeth would have been prepared for the exam if she

    _____ (listen) to the lectures last week.

4. As I typed my research paper yesterday morning, my roommate's

    cocker spaniel _____ (sit) by my chair.

5. After my grandparents' television set was repaired,

    their stereo _____ (break) down.

Chapter 35   Exercise A
Agreement

Each of these sentences is correct. Read the sentences carefully and explain why each verb form is used in each case.

Example: *Pride and Prejudice* provides valuable insights about life in nineteenth-century England.

(The verb is singular because the subject *Pride and Prejudice* is a title of an individual work, even though it is plural in form.)

1.   The children in the audience were mesmerized by the magician's entertaining illusions.

_____

_____

2.   Mr. Reidinger's confidence in the benefits of Scouting activities has convinced him to serve as the scoutmaster, even though his son is no longer in the troop.

_____

_____

3.   One look at their faces tells you that Angela and Erica enjoy playing softball.

_____

_____

Chapter 35   Exercise B
Agreement

Each of these sentences is correct. Read the sentences carefully and explain why each verb form is used in each case.

Example: *Pride and Prejudice* provides valuable insights about life in nineteenth-century England.

(The verb is singular because the subject *Pride and Prejudice* is a title of an individual work, even though it is plural in form.)

1. Although he fishes often with great success, Mr. Mims seldom comes home with a stringer because he considers "catch and release" to be sportsmanlike.

_____

_____

2. Every coach and player was pleased that the thunderstorm quickly passed through the area.

_____

_____

3. Aerodynamics is extremely important to bicycle design.

_____

_____

Name _____ Date _____ Score _____

Chapter 35   Exercise C
Agreement

Write "C" if the sentence is correct or "X" if it contains an error in agreement. Rewrite incorrect sentences so that subjects and verbs agree.

_____ 1. They make good pizza here.

_____ 2. Everybody know how to work together.

_____ 3. The thunder and lightning was frightening.

_____ 4. Either of the doctors can perform the surgery.

_____ 5. Neither of the animals have been fed.

_____ 6. Each member of the team has a uniform.

_____ 7. You was an excellent worker on that project.

_____ 8. Can you believe the pizzas was late?

Chapter 35   Exercise D
Agreement

On your own paper, rewrite the following passage, changing the subject from a carpenter to carpenters. Keep in mind that verbs and other words that refer to the subject will have to be changed from singular to plural.

A carpenter uses many different tools in his work. When he is faced with a job that is particularly difficult, he has to use his patience as well as his skill. Without patience, a hammer, a saw, or a screwdriver will do a carpenter no good. He has to be able to understand the problem, and find the best way to solve it. Sometimes, the quickest solution is not the best one. His customer, or client, has to be pleased with his work, or he loses his chance to be hired for another job. There is a great pressure on the carpenter to succeed. By no means is his job an easy one.

Chapter 35   Exercise E
Agreement

Double underline the antecedent for the underlined pronoun in each sentence.

1. Leigh used <u>her</u> pen to write in her notebook.

2. Don wore a jacket over <u>his</u> sweatshirt.

3. Everyone at the party enjoyed <u>her</u> evening.

4. The car has a leak in <u>its</u> transmission.

5. The cow twitched <u>its</u> tail at the fly.

6. Aunt Peggy asked me to catch <u>her</u> dog.

7. My sister earned <u>her</u> doctorate at Florida State.

8. After Grace concluded her recital, the audience applauded <u>her</u> performance and hoped for an encore.

9. During winter snowstorms, the sparrows depend on our feeder for <u>their</u> food.

10. The rain fell throughout the afternoon; by supper, though, <u>it</u> had stopped, so we did not cancel our plans for the evening.

Chapter 35   Exercise F
Agreement

Complete each sentence by underlining the word or phrase that fits logically and clearly.

1. Thirty students have submitted (his / their) lab proposals.

2. Seconds later, Reece grabbed (its / his) backpack and ran.

3. With the hat, Andy wore (her / its) decorative headband.

4. Meg bakes bread that only (her / its) mother can rival.

5. Is Luke's car running (their / its) best this week?

6. My dog sleeps in (its / their) own cozy bed in the garage.

7. Idea became reality when Thomas used (its / his) brain.

8. Of the boys, Nat is most likely to have (his / their) work.

9. Spectacular views are Ronnie's goal on (his / their) hike.

10. Pleasure and confidence are (its / their) own rewards.

Chapter 36   Exercise A
Adjectives and Adverbs

Underline the adjectives in the following sentences.

1. Clean air is essential if we are to have a safe environment.

2. On the lunar horizon, earth looms blue and cloud-streaked.

3. Whose car did you drive in this relentless downpour?

4. Lost and frightened children always arouse public sympathy.

5. This answer is correct, but that one is not.

6. Although his hair was gray, he was younger than he looked.

7. Did you leave your red umbrella at my house?

8. She was much taller than I.

9. His rumpled clothes and muddy shoes suggested that he had been
    walking for a long time.

10. The theater was crowded as the first showing ended.

Chapter 36   Exercise B
Adjectives and Adverbs

Complete each sentence by underlining the correct adverb in parentheses.

Example: The artful dodger dodged (<u>more artfully</u> / more artfullier) than the pursuer.

1. The (unique / most unique) shop opened last month.

2. Her embroidery is always (more delicate / more delicatest) than anyone else's.

3. Cindy became (more sick / more sickly) as the cruise continued into its third day.

4. Lynn is the (taller / tallest) of the two roommates.

5. Andy is (heavier / heaviest) than any other member of the state championship wrestling team.

6. Andy is the (heavier / heaviest) member of the state championship wrestling team.

7. David didn't act (grateful / gratefully) for the help.

8. Mocha is the (younger / youngest) of the six pups.

9. Ashley ran a (faster / more fast) mile than anyone else at the region track meet.

10. This unexpected winter storm is now (worse / badder) than it was an hour ago.

Review Exercise A for Part 6, Chapters 32–36
Understanding Grammar

In the space provided, revise the following student draft to correct errors in pronoun use. Change words and phrases as necessary.

Duck, Duck, Goose is a game that children play on a flat surface, usually outside in the grass so you do not get hurt. The first thing you need to do is to put them in a circle so them are sitting down. Choose one to be "it." They will be the first player to choose the "goose." The child whom is "it" will then go around the circle and tap everyone on the head. "It" will say "duck" when they tap them on the head except when they reach one—anyone who they choose. They will tap them on they head and say "goose."

_____

_____

_____

_____

_____

_____

_____

(This exercise continues on the next page.)

That's when the excitement begins. The "goose" will get up and chase "it" around the outside of the circle until they reach the place where "goose" was sitting and sits down. If "goose" tags "it" before "it" reaches the place where he was sitting, then they have to sit in the middle of the circle that they have made until someone else is tagged by a different "goose." When all of them have had the chance to be the "goose" and "it," then it can end.

_____

_____

_____

_____

_____

_____

_____

_____

Review Exercise B for Part 6, Chapters 32–36
Understanding Grammar

On your own paper, revise the following student draft to eliminate incorrect, inconsistent, or ineffective verb use. Change words and phrases as necessary.

Mocha the Wonder Dog

On April 6, 1990, Mocha, my cocker spaniel, was born. Six months following her birth, I begun to train Mocha with Mr. Cowart, a professional dog trainer. After two weeks of obedience training, Mocha learned the "Heel" and "Sit" commands. We worked for four more weeks, spending thirty minutes a day on more basic obedience commands. Mocha, of course, responds very well. Not only she learned all of the obedience commands, but she and I had also built a strong relationship. We were best friends.

I felt good about what I had done with Mocha and how all of those obedience commands had been learned by her. Mocha and I continued to work with one another even after the classes ended. During that time, she starts doing things that I had nothing to do with. For some reason, she likes to chase cars that driven on the street in front of our house.

(This exercise continues on the next page.)

Review Exercise B for Part 6, Chapters 32–36 (continued)
Understanding Grammar

On a hot summer day, a tragedy happens. My father is coming down the driveway in a different truck. Mocha hadn't really recognized who was driving the truck or the truck itself, so she darts out in front of it, trying to make it slow down before entering the yard. Unfortunately, the right front wheel hits Mocha in the hind leg and the right back wheel hit her in the head.

Fortunately, Mocha was still alive! No one was allowed to help her but me. Scared to death, I picked her up and she was put in the back of the truck. My dad rushed Mocha and me to the animal hospital. Mocha's blood is all over my hands and shirt, but I didn't care. All I want was for Mocha has the best medical care possible. Nearly crying, I lifted Mocha back out of the truck and take her inside the animal hospital.

After four days of treatment, the veterinarians allow me to take Mocha home, provided that she would be kept under close supervision. Limping away from the veterinarians, Mocha is eager to get home. It took another two weeks before she has totally healed. After her recovery was made, we continued her training, and she has made even more astonishing accomplishments. I am so proud of Mocha! Now that I am in college I miss her very much, but she will be seen again when I go home.

160

Chapter 37   Exercise A
Using End Punctuation

Correct these sentences by adding missing periods and by deleting unnecessary periods.

Example: Julius Caesar was killed in 44 B.C..

Julius Caesar was killed in 44 B.C.

1. Students are sometimes confused by the graduation requirements for the AA, the AS, and the AAS

_____

_____

2. Having gone through rigorous training at the Malcolm M Adamson facilities in St Petersburg, they were prepared now for their work in the Peace Corps

_____

_____

3. In the June 2000 issue of the *J.A.M.A.* is an interesting paper summarizing Dr W Dan Drinnon's recent research on D.N.A..

_____

_____

Chapter 37   Exercise B
Using End Punctuation

Correct these sentences by adding missing periods and by deleting unnecessary periods.

Example: Julius Caesar was killed in 44 B.C..

Julius Caesar was killed in 44 B.C.

1. Supreme Court Justice Sample's speech at the ABA convention was scheduled for 10 am, but it was postponed until 2 pm

_____

_____

2. This C.D.-R.O.M. has more memory than all the R.A.M. that was on the first computer that I owned.

_____

_____

3. After Beth graduated from F.S.U. with a J.D, she interviewed with N.A.S.A. in Florida and with the J.P.L. in California.

_____

_____

Chapter 37   Exercise C
Using End Punctuation

Correct the use of question marks in the following sentences. If a sentence needs no changes, write *correct*.

Example: Are they really going to China??!!

            Are they really going to China?

1. Marion asked whether the game had been postponed because of the thunderstorm?

_____

_____

2. Are they really going to jump from that bridge???

_____

_____

3. In his disgust, Stuart asked, "Will this rain ever end?"?

_____

_____

Chapter 37   Exercise D
Using End Punctuation

Correct the use of exclamation points in these sentences.

Example: This is fantastic. I can't believe you bought this for me.

This is fantastic! I can't believe you bought this for me.

1.   Are you kidding?! I never said that.

_____

_____

2.   Caught up in the excitement of the game, the announcer shouted, "What a spectacular shot."

_____

_____

3.   Wow!! Just what I always wanted!! A red Mustang!!

_____

_____

Chapter 38   Exercise A
Using Commas

In the space provided, write "C" if the sentence is punctuated correctly or "X" if it contains an error in comma usage.

1. _____ They went to London, where they saw the queen.

2. _____ I called my sister last night and told her that I might be

late for Thanksgiving dinner but I would be there before sunset.

3. _____ Before Alexandra knew it, the game was over.

4. _____ Until Matt decides to study, he will continue to fail.

5. _____ After he decides to study his grades will begin to improve.

6. _____ Although the salary is low, Richard likes to work.

7. _____ Although Cliff was much in debt, he entered the bank with

the air of a conqueror.

8. _____ Kelsey tore up her first three drafts, because she wanted the

letter to be perfect.

9. _____ The parlor, large and luxurious, was beautifully furnished.

10. _____ An beautiful parrot, with colorful plumage, played the

piano and sang three ballads.

Chapter 38   Exercise B
Using Commas

Insert any missing commas.

Example: My opinion inasmuch as you asked is that the expedition
is likely to succeed.

My opinion, inasmuch as you asked, is that the expedition
is likely to succeed.

1. Beth's report made it clear that her four favorite artists are Monet
Renoir Degas and Manet.

2. Let Brian and Angela our most skillful speakers present our
proposal to the board of directors.

3. Long regarded as a leading newspaper the *Washington Post* boasts
an outstanding staff of reporters.

4. Slowly slyly and cautiously Eric slid the wallet across the kitchen
table.

5. During Louie's sophomore year in high school he read *As You
Like It Julius Caesar Romeo and Juliet* and *Hamlet*.

6. I believe that is the book.

7. I believe that but it is an unusual excuse.

8. I believe that a dozen eggs will make quite a mess.

9. The elephant that stands on the drum is Maggie.

10. The elephant which is a hard worker and a talented performer is
found in most zoos and circuses.

Name _____ Date _____ Score _____

Chapter 38   Exercise C
Using Commas

The following sentences contain errors in the use of commas. Insert a comma as necessary. Circle any comma that should be deleted.

1. Once upon a time there was a dog that could fly.

2. We met as usual at the corner of Hollywood, and Vine.

3. I waited, for nearly a month for your letter.

4. It is my choice however to travel alone.

5. For once try studying.

6. You are mine and I am yours.

7. Write to me at 65 Market Street Portland Maine.

8. You are all prepared I'm sure for the test.

9. Ice cream if it is made at home is very good.

10. As long as I live I will love to dance.

Chapter 38   Exercise D
Using Commas

The following sentences contain errors in the use of commas. Insert a comma as necessary. Circle any comma that should be deleted.

1. Waving her wand the good fairy performed some magic.

2. Never never will you get away with that.

3. I had a bacon lettuce and tomato sandwich for lunch.

4. Who in your opinion is the world's greatest athlete?

5. Her latest poem, is superb.

6. As of next week the prisoner will be a free man.

7. His answer which was wrong made the class laugh.

8. That dog barking at the tree, is mine.

9. We were wed on March 18 1939.

10. When our guests arrived we greeted them at the door.

Chapter 39   Exercise A
Using Semicolons

Replace commas with semicolons where necessary to separate internally punctuated items in a series.

Example: The Aleutian Islands, located off the west coast of Alaska, are an extremely remote chain of islands, they are sometimes called America's Siberia.

The Aleutian Islands, located off the west coast of Alaska, are an extremely remote chain of islands; they are sometimes called America's Siberia.

1. Business letters should be written with a personal, courteous tone, best achieved through the use of the word *you*, a positive tone, easily created by rephrasing negative statements, and a natural tone, the result of using language that is intended to express, not impress.

_____

_____

2. Engaging in aerobic exercise results in benefits to the cardiovascular system, an increase in stamina, an important physical asset in today's fast-paced lifestyle, and an overall sense of well-being.

_____

_____

Name _____ Date _____ Score _____

Chapter 39   Exercise B
Using Semicolons

Combine each of the following sentence groups into one sentence that contains only two independent clauses. Use a semicolon to separate the two clauses. You may need to add, delete, relocate, or change some words; keep experimenting until you find the arrangement that best conveys the meaning of the group of sentences. Your answers may vary from the model answer.

Example: In the springtime, birds nest in the fir tree in my back yard. I see fluttering chickadees. I see bold cardinals.

In the springtime, birds nest in the fir tree in my backyard; I see fluttering chickadees and bold cardinals.

1.   Television soap operas provide a diversion to real life. Soap opera characters are often wealthy. The never seem to work.

_____

_____

2.   Ads on afternoon soap operas are directed primarily toward women. The viewer rarely sees ads for men on afternoon soap operas. These ads include soap, toothpaste, skin creams, and nail products.

_____

_____

Chapter 39   Exercise C
Using Semicolons

Combine each of the following sentence groups into one sentence that contains only two independent clauses. Use a semicolon to separate the two clauses. You may need to add, delete, relocate, or change some words; keep experimenting until you find the arrangement that best conveys the meaning of the group of sentences. Your answers may vary from the model answer.

Example: In the springtime, birds nest in the dogwood tree in my back yard. I see fluttering chickadees. I see bold cardinals.

In the springtime, birds nest in the dogwood tree in my backyard; I see fluttering chickadees and bold cardinals.

1.   Hale-Bopp was an extraordinary comet. It was seen by millions of ordinary people. It was visible at sunrise and sunset in the spring of 1997 throughout the United States.

_____

_____

2.   The United States Capitol is at one end of the Mall. The Washington Monument is at the other end. Both visitors and residents use the space between the two for volleyball, sunbathing, and strolling.

_____

_____

Chapter 39   Exercise D
Using Semicolons

Combine each of the following sentence groups into one sentence that includes a series of items separated by semicolons. You may need to add, delete, relocate, or change words. Try several versions of each sentence until you find the most effective arrangement.

Example: The flag of each Scandinavian country depicts a cross on a solid background. Denmark's flag is red with a white cross. Norway's flag is also red, but its cross is blue, outlined in white. Sweden's flag is blue with a yellow cross.

The flag of each Scandinavian country depicts a cross on a solid background: Denmark's flag is red with a white cross; Norway's flag is also red, but its cross is blue, outlined in white; and Sweden's flag is blue with a yellow cross.

1.   Research on animals' ability to think has been conducted on dolphins, who often respond to communicative gestures, sea lions, who seem to show some understanding of logical relationships between symbols, and parrots, who can be taught vocabulary.

_____

_____

2.   Through his computer-enhanced classroom lectures, Dr. Riser took his students around the world: they visited the pyramids of Giza, guarded by the Sphynx, they climbed the Acropolis, where they walked among the Parthenon's ruins, and they heard the choirs of the Gothic cathedrals, including Chartres and Lyon.

_____

_____

Chapter 40   Exercise A
Using Apostrophes

Insert missing apostrophes in the following sentences.

Example: Its a shame that your ring is lost.

It's a shame that your ring is lost.

1. Im not going out in that blizzard.

2. Have you corrected Karens homework yet?

3. Genes store specializes in mens clothing.

4. Allens store carries only boys clothes.

5. My brother-in-laws job is with the county clerks office.

6. Frances and Englands agreement was offset by Japans secret pact

   with Germany.

7. Watch your Ps and Qs at Grandmas house.

8. Johns condition results entirely from neglect.

9. Bev is going on a weeks vacation.

10. Well go if youll stay with the baby.

Chapter 40   Exercise B
Using Apostrophes

Insert missing apostrophes in the following sentences.

Example: Wheres the monkeys toy?

Where's the monkey's toy?

1. Im just a person who cant say no.

2. The childs role is to play the Spirit of 76.

3. His bachelors degree is from his countrys only university.

4. Tally the Ys here and the Ns there.

5. Oohs and ahs rose from the astonished audience.

6. For an hours labor, Lochlin earned a days pay.

7. I wanted to hear yess, but all I heard were maybes.

8. Does Sarah know her ABCs already?

9. The Cowarts home is just around the corner.

10. Amys apartment is upstairs; Jessicas is downstairs.

11. What will the class of 73 plan for the reunion?

12. The five partners signatures were necessary.

13. Shes home, but hes working at a childrens camp.

14. "Well, well have to honor his last will if were to divide the estate now," said the attorney.

Chapter 41   Exercise A
Using Quotation Marks

Insert missing quotation marks or other related punctuation in the sentences that follow.

1. Where do you think you're going she demanded.

2. Yogi Berra said It ain't over till its over.

3. "A Philmont Experience" is the cover story in the June edition of

   Scouter Magazine.

4. Can you Yanks tell me said the British officer where to find your

   commanding officer

5. Hemingways *Men without Women* included the story In Another

   Country.

6. Dover Beach is one of Matthew Arnold's best-known poems.

7. Who said Yes

8. Open your blue books said the professor and begin your exam.

9. The rain has ruined our ski trip complained Megan.

10. We will meet again in two weeks said the professor as the class

    began to leave.

Chapter 41   Exercise B
Using Quotation Marks

Add single and double quotation marks to these sentences where necessary to set off direct quotations from identifying tags.

Example: William Congreve wrote, Heaven has no rage like love to hatred turned, / Nor hell a fury like a woman scorned.

William Congreve wrote, "Heaven has no rage like love to hatred turned, / Nor hell a fury like a woman scorned."

1. Why in the world, asked Amanda in her customary frantic manner, would you think that I'm annoyed by the dent that suddenly appeared in the fender?

2. To many freshmen, social security means a date for Saturday night.

3. Christopher Marlowe posed this question about Helen of Troy: Was this the face that launched a thousand ships, / And burnt the topless towers of Ilium?

4. *Aggravate* means to worsen, while *irritate* means to annoy.

5. If you'll submit your research paper one week early, announced Professor Davis, I'll give you ten percent extra credit, and you won't have to take the term examination.

Chapter 42   Exercise A
Using Other Punctuation Marks

Circle the correct punctuation mark given in the parentheses.

1. I have never been to England (; / :) it is supposed to be lovely.

2. It is lovely in three seasons (; / :) spring, summer, and fall.

3. Winter is not so lovely (; / :) it is cold and windy then.

4. It may be cold, and it may snow (; / :) nevertheless, I can have fun in the winter.

5. In winter I enjoy the following (; / :) skiing, skating, and tobogganing.

6. I also like summer sports (; / :) swimming, riding, hiking.

7. Winter in England is the time for sleigh rides (; / :) summer is the time for hayrides.

8. I used to enjoy staying home (; / :) now I would like to travel.

9. I would enjoy visiting many lands (; / :) France, England, Italy, Norway, Switzerland.

10. There are two pleasures to traveling (; / :) seeing new faces, and visiting new places.

Chapter 42   Exercise B
Using Other Punctuation Marks

Correct any errors in the use of semicolons or colons. Insert your corrections within the paragraph.

The team was in trouble, it had dropped from first place to last in three weeks. The manager called a meeting of the players at which the following issues were discussed; the importance of developing a winning attitude, whereby the players would place the goals of the team over their individual achievements, the imposition of a strict curfew so that the players would be well rested for the games, the problem of teammates competing among themselves for higher salaries and greater coverage in the newspapers, and last but not least, the general lack of hustle and determination on the part of the team's stars.

Chapter 42   Exercise C
Using Other Punctuation Marks

Add dashes where needed in the following sentences.

Example: World War I called "the war to end all wars" was, unfortunately, no such thing.

World War I—called "the war to end all wars"—was, unfortunately, no such thing.

1. Scuba self-contained underwater breathing apparatus is widely known as an equipment-intensive sport.

2. Scuba enthusiasts have a variety of reasons a background in snorkeling, an admiration for marine life, and an interest in underwater formations for becoming certified divers.

3. The basic snorkeling equipment mask, fin, and snorkel are also essential to scuba diving.

4. The economies of Cayman Brac, Belize, and Dominica three of the Western Hemisphere's most popular scuba diving destinations depend on tourism.

5. For two reasons very important to us observing marine life at forty feet below the surface and eating seafood at a popular restaurant back on shore our family enjoys taking scuba vacations.

Chapter 42   Exercise D
Using Other Punctuation Marks

Add parentheses where needed in the following sentences.

Example: The greatest battle of the War of 1812 the Battle of New
            Orleans was fought after the war was declared over.

            The greatest battle of the War of 1812 (the Battle of New
            Orleans) was fought after the war was declared over.

1. George Orwell's *1984* 1949 focuses on the dangers of a totalitarian

    society.

2. The final score 56-0 was a devastating blow for the Wildcats.

3. Hoyt told us that Belize formerly British Honduras offers

    spectacular off-shore diving opportunities.

4. The first phonics book *Phonics Is Fun* has a bright blue cover.

5. Some high school students participate in so many extracurricular

    activities band, sports, drama club, and school newspaper, for

    instance that they have little time to study.

Chapter 43   Exercise A
Capitalization

Correct any capitalization errors—lower-case letters that should be capitals or capitals that should be lower case.

              aunt   February

Example: My Aunt always gets depressed in february.

1. The Professor who taught english 202 changed my attitude about reading the Poetry of alexander pope and robert frost.

2. Swedish tennis pro Bjorn Borg, who won the wimbledon title that year, lost the U.S. Open Championship at flushing meadow stadium.

3. When Whitney was at harvard, I used to take the amtrak train to Boston every friday to visit her.

4. The statue of liberty was closed when i was in new york, but i still took the Ferry boat to ellis island.

5. The Articles of Confederation preceded the constitution of the United States and the bill of rights.

Chapter 43   Exercise B
Capitalization

Correct any capitalization errors—lower-case letters that should be capitals or capitals that should be lower case.

Lucky Chance Grill

Example: Working at the lucky chance grill has educated me

human nature

about Human Nature.

1. When Fall arrives, the children—angela, erica, beth, and brian—begin to plan for halloween.

2. We drove up maple street until we came to the Highway and turned North toward cumberland state park.

3. Professor andrew luke thomas explained that Siddhartha, called the buddha, founded buddhism in india.

4. Many americans faced hard times when the roaring twenties gave way to the great depression.

5. Our assignment is to read george eliot's *middlemarch*.

6. The mayflower compact established a government for plymouth colony.

7. On a clear Summer evening, we can see the big dipper in the sky.

Chapter 44   Exercise A
Italics

Underline any words that should be italicized.

Example: Year after year, new parents turn to Dr. Spock's <u>Baby and</u>
<u>Child Care</u>.

1. Because it is extremely challenging, William Faulkner's <u>The</u>
<u>Sound and the Fury</u> is one of those novels that I have enjoyed
reading multiple times.

2. Lincoln first gave his Gettysburg Address at the dedication of a
cemetery.

3. For many people, the word <u>cavalry</u> is a tongue twister.

4. When the Supreme Court decided <u>Marbury</u> v. <u>Madison</u>, it
established the right of judicial review.

5. The hero of <u>Beowulf</u>, a long epic poem in Old English, dies
fighting a dragon.

6. <u>The Thinker</u> is Rodan's best-known sculpture.

7. When <u>Sesame Street</u> was first broadcast, it challenged conventional
ideas about children's television.

8. The drama group presented Shakespeare's <u>Romeo and Juliet</u> in
modern dress.

9. She can call him or <u>vice versa</u>.

10. <u>Cyperus papyrus</u> was used in ancient Egypt for fuel, food, fabric,
and paper.

Chapter 44   Exercise B
Italics

Underline any words that should be italicized.

Example: Year after year, new parents turn to Dr. Spock's <u>Baby and</u>
<u>Child Care</u>.

1. I always have trouble pronouncing the word schism.

2. He wrote there, but he meant their.

3. She call is strombis pugilis; I call it a pretty shell.

4. I read the Los Angeles Times every day, but I also like the weekly
    coverage in Newsweek.

5. Stadman's article on Dutch Protestantism appeared in the
    Sixteenth Century Journal.

6. A similar argument, "Patterns of Worship in Flanders," appeared
    in Renaissance Studies.

7. An Atlantic crossing on a Concorde is nothing like one was on the
    Mayflower.

8. The word canteen, derived from the Italian cantina, has been used
    in English since the eighteenth century.

9. The giant panda, Ailuropoda melanoleuca, is related not to the
    bear but to the raccoon.

10. The choir presents Handel's Messiah each year.

Chapter 45   Exercise A
Hyphens

Form compound adjectives from the following word groups, inserting hyphens where necessary.

Example: a contract for three years

a three-year contract

1.   the football game between Army and Navy

_____

2.   a computer whiz who is age twelve

_____

3.   a hard drive with eighty gigabytes

_____

4.   a majority of two of three votes

_____

5.   a painting completed during the eighteenth century

_____

Chapter 45   Exercise B
Hyphens

Add hyphens to the compounds in these sentences wherever they are necessary. Consult a dictionary if necessary.

Example: Alaska was the forty ninth state to join the United States.
            Alaska was the forty-ninth state to join the United States.

1. My pre certification class has fifty three students on the roster, but only thirty seven have shown up.

2. By emphasizing her position as a middle of the road independent, the little known candidate hopes to win the runoff.

3. One of the restaurant's blue plate specials is chicken fried steak.

4. Both Texas and Virginia are right to work states.

5. Don stood on tiptoe to see the near perfect statue, which was well hidden by the security fence.

6. The new store in the mall has a self service makeup counter and stocks many up to the minute gadgets.

7. The so called Saturday night special is opposed by pro gun control groups.

8. For his pre-game meal, he ordered two all beef patties with special sauce, lettuce, cheese, pickles, and onions on a sesame seed bun for his pre game meal.

9. Although last night's speaker presented some thought provoking insights, he hardly presented any earth shattering conclusions.

10. The Braves Mets game was rained out, so the long suffering fans left for home.

Chapter 46   Exercise A
Abbreviations

In the space provided below each sentence, correct any abbreviations that should be spelled out or any words that would be abbreviated in an essay.

1. Of the three bros., Wm. Collins, Junior, is obviously tallest, standing 6 ft. 11 ins. in his stocking feet.

   _____

2. In his address to the Corps of Cadets last Thurs., Gen. Ross announced a 12% increase in dessert expenditures.

   _____

3. Although Meg mailed the two letters on the same day at an Atlanta post office, she was surprised that one letter arrived in CA two days before the other arrived in FL.

   _____

4. Following the announcement that he had been named this year's winner of the Nobel Prize in Lit., Prof. Jim Riser received congratulatory telephone calls from several of his former colleagues: Dr. Bertram Davis in Lake George, NY; from Gov. John Fenstermaker in Columbus, OH; and from Sen. Anne Rowe in Tallahassee, FL.

   _____

5. After taking my bus. admin. final exam, I returned to my dorm room & found a note that read, "See you this aft. when yr. tests are thru."

   _____

Chapter 46   Exercise B
Abbreviations

In the space provided below each sentence, correct any abbreviations that should be spelled out or any words that would be abbreviated in an essay.

1. Saint Valentine, martyred c. 270, is remembered thru-out the world each year on Feb. 14.

_____

2. When it is 1 p.m. EST, it is only 11 a.m. MST.

_____

3. With her M.A., Beth intends to teach at the local jr. coll. for a few years, but she hopes to earn her doctorate so she can move to a major univ. near her hometown in TN.

_____

_____

4. That section of Intro. to Shakespeare meets Mon., Wed., & Fri. at 11 a.m. in the Gabehart Memorial Bldg.

_____

_____

5. Today I have anthro. at 8 a.m., but my 10 a.m. lit. course has been canceled, so I hope to get some Xmas shopping done before I work my aft. noon shift.

_____

_____

Chapter 47   Exercise A
Numbers

In the space provided below each sentence, correct any numbers that are not treated according to the conventions for nonscientific writing.

1. Including taxes, the price came to nine thousand five hundred twenty dollars and thirty-four cents.

_____

2. My office number is two thirty-four; I'm usually there and working at the computer by nine a.m.

_____

3. In eighteen hundred cc of nitrogen, we dissolved three hundred fifty-four point nine gm of liquid sodium.

_____

4. Physics one twenty-five meets on Thursday mornings.

_____

5. On page six, the author cites a 12 percent increase in revenues for fiscal year nineteen hundred seventy-one.

_____

6. The experiment began at six-oh-six; 15 cc were added to the solution every 5 minutes.

_____

Chapter 47   Exercise B
Numbers

In the space provided below each sentence, correct any numbers that are
not treated according to the conventions for nonscientific writing.

1. Lindsay moved from twelve Sycamore Lane to Sixteen-B Windsor
    Road, just past Interstate Seventy-Five.

    _____

2. On June eight, nineteen hundred eighty-five, I made my final
    tuition payment of five hundred forty-seven dollars.

    _____

3. Dinner will be served about 7.

    _____

4. Breakfast ends at exactly nine a.m.

    _____

5. Of the 619 names on the mailing list, 309 submitted the
    questionnaire by the deadline (which was March nine, 1998), but
    only twenty-two responded to every question.

    _____

6. The restaurant is at 77 17th Avenue; I'll plan to meet you there no
    later than 1 o'clock on April sixth, 1990.

    _____

Review Exercise A for Part 7, Chapters 37–42
Understanding Punctuation

On your own paper, rewrite the following passage, inserting or revising periods, commas, exclamation points, question marks, and quotation marks.

Three men were stationed in the farthest reaches of Alaska, and their supply of orange juice was running low. Two of the men felt that they could take advantage of the third, so they told him to go out into the blizzard and buy some more orange juice in the nearest town. The third man said I will go only if you promise to save the last drop of this remaining orange juice for me. Don't worry the others said we promise. I will definitely not go if you drink that last drop the third man said. We promise, we promise, the others assured him. With that, the third man left. A day went by Two days went by A week and then two weeks went by. The two men figured that the third must have died in the blizzard so they decided "to drink the last bit of orange juice." They took the bottle from the refrigerator, said Cheers, and were about to indulge when the third man flung the door open. I told you he announced I wasn't going to go if you drank that last drop!

Review Exercise B for Part 7, Chapters 37–42
Understanding Punctuation

On your own paper, rewrite the following paragraphs so that they are properly punctuated.

Small towns and cities especially older ones face difficult financial problems Their revenues are limited but they're expected to maintain service levels despite added costs Sometimes the size of a towns annual budget is restricted by the state in other cases the local officials determine its size Ultimately such budgets are limited by the ability and willingness of citizens to pay the property taxes that generally fund such municipalities.

When a municipal budget is strained officials have two choices increase revenues or cut expenditures In the past extra funds came from the state and federal governments but now many towns must do without such aid Instead increased revenues can come only from new homes whose owners pay property taxes new or revitalized businesses whose tax bills rise with their revenues or new industry whose taxes are a function of space occupied and revenues.

In an older town however with little vacant land not much new growth can be encouraged In addition revitalizing an old run down business district requires time capital and community support Thus if revenues cant or dont grow towns have no choice but to cut their expenses.

How can a town or small city spend less One city manager summed up the problem when he said Were like a business during tough times We have to be more efficient more careful with our pennies and more concerned about our customers the demanding overburdened taxpayers who depend on our services And how does a town accomplish this Few communities have long-term answers for many fixed costs pensions utilities insurance and the like are beyond their control.

Review Exercise C for Part 7, Chapters 43–47
Spelling and Mechanics

Read the following sentences, looking for errors in spelling, capitalization, and hyphenation, and for misuse of italics, abbreviations, and numbers. In the space provided, write corrected forms of the following sentences.

1. After Mr Campbell asked for a dozen workers to assist with the Craft Fair at the nursing home, over 30 members of boy scout troop 172 volunteered because they enjoyed working with the residents at last year's event.

   _____

   _____

   _____

   _____

2. The scouts also know that mr campbell will reward them by cooking his specialty—Turkey and dressing dinner—on the next camping trip.

   _____

   _____

   _____

(This exercise continues on the next page.)

Review Exercise C for Part 7, Chapters 43–47 (continued)
Spelling and Mechanics

3. The 3 wk unit of study culminated with Mr Hansard's dramatic reading of tennyson's famous poem, *The Charge of the Light Brigade*, accompanied by the overture from the Rossini's opera, William Tell.

4. When Mr Estabrook announced the expenses for last month's camporee (sixty five thousand eight hundred and fifty dollars), Mr Flerchinger was so startled that he almost fell out of his chair.

Review Exercise D for Part 7, Chapters 43–47
Spelling and Mechanics

Read the following sentences, looking for errors in spelling, capitalization, and hyphenation, and for misuse of italics, abbreviations, and numbers. In the space provided, write corrected forms of the following sentences.

1. Although the calendar said January, it was a surprisingly warm, spring like thurs. morning—January 28th, to be exact—and all andrew could think about was how he would celebrate his birthday with his brothers.

   _____

   _____

   _____

   _____

2. Luke earned a four year scholarship to the Fla. public college of his choice; his goal is to earn an m.a. & then choose a grad. school where he can earn a Doctorate.

   _____

   _____

   _____

(This exercise continues on the next page.)

3. One of the most famous of eighteenth century literary pieces is Jonathan swift's gulliver's travels, which we read in our English Twenty-Two Ten class last semester.

_____

_____

_____

_____

4. The local teachers' union negotiated an excellent contract; each teacher will have twenty seven paid holidays—including two weeks during the christmas break; one week for the easter break; and her birthday, plus the day before and the day after.

_____

_____

_____

_____

Name _____ Date _____ Score _____

Chapter 48   Exercise A
Understanding the Disciplines

Respond to each of the following based on the assumption that you will write an essay in the Humanities.

1. Identify three disciplines included among the Humanities.

_____

_____

_____

2. Identify three categories of research sources you should consult.

_____

_____

_____

3. Identify three categories of assignments your instructor might use.

_____

_____

_____

Name _____ Date _____ Score _____

Chapter 48   Exercise B
Understanding the Disciplines

Respond to each of the following based on the assumption that you will write an essay in the Social Sciences.

1. Identify three disciplines included among the Social Sciences.

_____

_____

_____

2. Identify three categories of research sources you should consult.

_____

_____

_____

3. Identify three categories of assignments your instructor might use.

_____

_____

_____

Chapter 49   Exercise A
Writing in the Humanities

Using one of the Web sites mentioned under the Art History or Music headings in section a3 Internet Sites of Chapter 49, identify five advantages that such a resource would provide as you conduct your research.

1. _____

_____

2. _____

_____

3. _____

_____

4. _____

_____

5. _____

_____

Chapter 49   Exercise B
Writing in the Humanities

Using one of the Web sites mentioned under the Drama or Film headings in section a3 Internet Sites of Chapter 49, identify five advantages that such a resource would provide as you conduct your research.

1. _____

_____

2. _____

_____

3. _____

_____

4. _____

_____

5. _____

_____

Chapter 50   Exercise A
Writing in the Social Sciences

Using one of the Web sites mentioned under the Political Science or Criminal Justice headings found in section a3 Internet Sites of Chapter 50, identify five advantages that such a resource would provide as you conduct your research.

1. _____

_____

2. _____

_____

3. _____

_____

4. _____

_____

5. _____

_____

Chapter 50   Exercise B
Writing in the Social Sciences

Using one of the Web sites mentioned under the Anthropology or
Business and Economics headings found in section a3 Internet Sites of
Chapter 50, identify five advantages that such a resource would provide
as you conduct your research.

1. _____

_____

2. _____

_____

3. _____

_____

4. _____

_____

5. _____

_____

Chapter 51   Exercise A
Writing in the Natural and Applied Sciences

Using one of the Web sites mentioned under the Physics or Earth Science headings found in section a3 Internet Sites of Chapter 51, identify five advantages that such a resource would provide as you conduct your research.

1. _____

   _____

2. _____

   _____

3. _____

   _____

4. _____

   _____

5. _____

   _____

Chapter 51   Exercise B
Writing in the Natural and Applied Sciences

Using one of the Web sites mentioned under the Biology or Life
Science headings found in section a3 Internet Sites of Chapter 51,
identify five advantages that such a resource would provide as you
conduct your research.

1. _____

_____

2. _____

_____

3. _____

_____

4. _____

_____

5. _____

_____

Chapter 52   Exercise A
Writing Essay Exams

Read each of the following essay exam topics and determine what kind of question it poses. Does it ask for comparison and contrast, division and classification, or cause and effect?

1. Discuss the most appealing characteristics that you find at three of your favorite campgrounds.

2. Discuss the consequences of poor preparation for a camping trip.

3. Identify the characteristics of three types of sleeping bags that you have considered owning.

4. Discuss the advantages and disadvantages of two pairs of hiking boots that you have considered purchasing.

5. Explain why you chose to hike forty-five miles of the Appalachian Trail during Spring Break, instead of accompanying your friends on their trip to Panama City Beach, Florida.

Chapter 52   Exercise B
Writing Essay Exams

Select three of the essay exam topics found in Exercise A. For each topic, compose the topic sentence that you might use to begin your essay response.

_____

_____

_____

_____

_____

_____

_____

_____

_____

_____

Chapter 53   Exercise A
Writing about Literature

Assume that your instructor has assigned an essay in which you are to provide a summary of the scholarly comments that have been written about *Hamlet* during the past ten years. Identify five credible sources that you would consider appropriate for your purposes.

1. _____

2. _____

3. _____

4. _____

5. _____

Chapter 53   Exercise B
Writing about Literature

Assume that your instructor has assigned an essay in which you are to provide a summary of the scholarly comments that have been written about *Hamlet* during the past ten years. Identify five unworthy sources that you would consider inappropriate for your purposes.

1. _____

2. _____

3. _____

4. _____

5. _____

Chapter 54   Exercise A
Writing for the Workplace

Think of a job that you would like to have ten years after you complete your college education. In the space below, provide a letter of application in the semiblock format. Continue the letter on the back of this page.

_____

_____

_____

_____

_____

_____

_____

_____

_____

(This exercise continues on the next page.)

Continue the letter of application in the space below.

_____

_____

_____

_____

_____

_____

_____

_____

_____

_____

Chapter 54   Exercise B
Writing for the Workplace

In the space below, provide a sample résumé in chronological order to accompany the letter of application you created in Exercise A. Remember that you will apply for this job ten years after you complete your college education. Feel free to embellish this résumé with entries that you hope to accomplish by then. Continue the résumé on the back of this page.

_____

_____

_____

_____

_____

_____

_____

_____

(This exercise continues on the next page.)

Continue the résumé in the space below.

_____

_____

_____

_____

_____

_____

_____

_____

_____

_____

Name _____ Date _____ Score _____

Chapter 55   Exercise A
Document Design and Manuscript Format

Assume that you are beginning the final version of your essay for submission. The area below is intended to represent the initial page of your essay. Based on the MLA Manuscript Guidelines, provide the appropriate information that would appear atop the first page, plus the title and the essay's first sentence. For your convenience, lines have been provided.

Name _____ Date _____ Score _____

Chapter 55   Exercise B
Document Design and Manuscript Format

Assume that you are preparing for submission the Works Consulted
page that will serve as page 6 when it accompanies your essay. The
area below is intended to represent the Works Consulted page for your
essay. Based on the MLA Manuscript Guidelines, provide the
appropriate information that would appear atop the Works Consulted
page, plus the first three entries. For your convenience, lines have been
provided.

Review Exercise A for Part 8, Chapter 52
Writing in the Disciplines

Prepare a personalized list of the most important considerations as you prepare for an essay exam.

1. _____

2. _____

3. _____

4. _____

5. _____

Name _____ Date _____ Score _____

Review Exercise B for Part 8, Chapters 48–53
Writing in the Disciplines

Prepare a personalized list of the most important considerations as you prepare to submit an essay.

1. _____

2. _____

3. _____

4. _____

5. _____

Chapter 56   Exercise A
ESL: Language Issues for International Students

1. Write one sentence in which three adjectives describe one noun.

   _____

   _____

2. Write one sentence in which two adverbs describe one verb.

   _____

   _____

3. Write one sentence that includes two prepositional phrases.

   _____

   _____

Chapter 56   Exercise B
ESL: Language Issues for International Students

Make a list of the most troublesome problems you face as you strive to increase your understanding of the English language.

_____

_____

_____

_____

_____

_____

_____

_____

_____

Chapter 57   Exercise A
A Glossary of Usage

Underline the correct word in the parentheses.

1. In ancient times, a comet signaled (eminent / imminent) danger.

2. The red convertible must have been going eighty miles per hour when it (passed / past) us on the freeway.

3. My dog (sits / sets) under our oak tree hoping to catch a squirrel.

4. The club's Code of Conduct embodies specific (principals / principles) that each member is expected to uphold.

5. After asking for clarification on the point, the judge directed the attorney to (precede / proceed).

6. Kenjy's grandparents (emigrated / immigrated) from Japan.

7. Laura's recovery seems much (farther / further) along than the doctors had anticipated.

8. While some people are convinced that Kentucky's (capital / capitol) is Louisville and others thinks it's Lexington, you'll have to visit Frankfort to find the governor in the (capital / capitol) building.

9. Although the retired general has (less / fewer) power than he once possessed, he's fortunate that he also has (less / fewer) worries and obligations.

10. Did you make a good grade on (your / you're) test?

Chapter 57   Exercise B
A Glossary of Usage

Underline the correct word in the parentheses.

1. Although your essay is three days late, your instructor will probably (accept / except) it, but she'll likely penalize it.

2. If you want the penalty to have less (affect / effect), you should submit the essay as soon as possible.

3. (Who's / Whose) team will win the tournament?

4. Dee's poem makes an (allusion / illusion) to the seven deadly sins.

5. (Its / It's) puzzling that Mitzi hasn't been seen for several days.

6. Most of your classmates confuse you and (your / you're) twin.

7. Lochlin provided a model for (their / they're / there) design.

8. The three parties agreed (among / between) themselves to settle the case.

9. Kelsey's gymnastics coach (complemented / complimented) her for showing excellent improvement.

10. Hoyt has requested to remain (conscience / conscious) throughout the entire procedure.

Answers to Selected Exercises

Note: Answers to half of the supplementary exercises are included in this Key. Answers to all exercises are included in the Instructor's Guide to *The Holt Handbook,* Sixth Edition.

PART 1 COMPOSING AN ESSAY

Chapter 1   Exercise B (p. 2)
Determining Your Purpose

Answers will vary. For this exercise, assign or have students choose a subject that can be developed into the first essay of the term.

Chapter 1   Exercise D (p. 4)
Freewriting

Answers will vary.

Chapter 1   Exercise F (p. 6)
Making a Cluster Diagram

Answers will vary. A student's first attempts at a cluster diagram may not be extremely well developed. With practice, though, your students should improve.

Chapter 2   Exercise B (p. 8)
Stating a Thesis

Answers will vary.

1. A husband can profoundly influence his wife by determining the location where they live, their social status, and their circle of friends.
2. The concerns over the viability of the social security system have caused Baby Boomers and younger generations to rethink the use of a multitude of savings vehicles for their retirement.

Chapter 2   Exercise D (p. 10)
Stating a Thesis

Answers will vary.

1. Cultural diversity has different meanings for many people.
2. Although the First Amendment guarantees freedom of speech, political correctness often inhibits its exercise.

Chapter 2   Exercise F (p. 12)
Preparing an Informal Outline

Answers will vary. Small-group discussion of informal outlines may be a useful classroom exercise.

Chapter 3   Exercise B (p. 14)
Collaborative Revision

Answers will vary. You might want to circulate among the teams to encourage constructive peer reviews, particularly if students are collaborating for the first time.

Chapter 4   Exercise B (p. 16)
Writer's Notebook: Composing an Essay

Answers will vary.

Chapter 5   Exercise B (p. 18)
Essay Patterns and Purposes

Answers will vary.

Chapter 6   Exercise B (p. 20)
Patterns of Paragraph Development

Answers will vary.

1. argumentation, classification, exemplification
2. cause and effect, exemplification, narration

3. argumentation, cause and effect, classification
4. argumentation, classification, exemplification
5. classification, exemplification

Chapter 6   Exercise D (p. 22)
Well-Developed Paragraphs

This paragraph could be further developed by enumeration of amounts of specific ingredients, types of containers, and utensils used. Baking times and temperatures can vary. Methods of storing and preserving the batter could be included. Flavoring and leavening are important ingredients to be discussed. Generally accepted bread-making procedures could be used as a guide for completing the process.

Chapter 7   Exercise B (p. 24)
Thinking Critically

Answers will vary.

Chapter 8   Exercise B (p. 26)
Thinking Logically

Answers will vary.

Chapter 9   Exercise B (p. 28)
Writing an Argumentative Essay

Answers will vary.

Review Exercise B for Part 1, Chapters 1–6 (p. 30)
Writing Essays and Paragraphs

Answers will vary.

The paragraph could be developed by using process analysis. It is important that the student present the steps of the planning process completely and in order. Students should remember to include appropriate warnings that will guide the reader to avoid issues that could undermine the effectiveness of the gathering.

Review Exercise D for Part 1, Chapters 7–9 (p. 32)
Critical Thinking and Argumentation

Answers will vary.

Chapter 10   Exercise B (p. 34)
Moving from Assignment to Topic

You might ask students to complete this exercise before or during a conference with you.

Chapter 10   Exercise D (p. 36)
Moving from Assignment to Topic

You might ask students to complete this exercise before or during a conference with you.

Chapter 10   Exercise F (p. 38)
Mapping Out a Search Strategy

You may need to advise students on the feasibility of keeping these reference lists on their computers.

Chapter 11   Exercise B (p. 40)
Evaluating Library Sources

You might provide a suitable article for students to work with, or you might want them to choose an article related to a subject they are writing about.

Chapter 12   Exercise B (p. 42)
Conducting a Keyword Search

Answers will vary.

Chapter 12   Exercise D (p. 44)
Using the Internet for Research

Answers will vary.

Chapter 13   Exercise B (p. 46)
Evaluating Web Sites

Answers will vary.

Chapter 13   Exercise D (p. 48)
Citing Electronic Sources

Answers will vary. Refer students to the MLA Documentation section in *The Holt Handbook*.

Chapter 14   Exercise B (p. 50)
Paraphrasing and Quoting

Answers will vary. Refer students to the MLA Documentation section in *The Holt Handbook*.

Chapter 14   Exercise D (p. 52)
Paraphrasing and Quoting

Answers will vary. Refer students to the MLA Documentation section in *The Holt Handbook*.

Chapter 15   Exercise B (p. 54)
Avoiding Plagiarism

1. Parenthetical citations
    Your students' citation will vary according to the requirements of each paragraph.
2. Answer will vary.
    Your students' citation will vary according to the requirements of each paragraph.

Chapter 16   Exercise B (p. 56)
MLA Documentation

Answers will vary.

Chapter 17   Exercise B (p. 58)
APA and Other Documentation Styles

Answers will vary.

Chapter 18   Exercise B (p. 60)
Research Notebook: A Student's Process

Answers will vary.

Review Exercise B for Part 2, Chapters 10–18 (p. 62)
Research

Answers will vary.

Review Exercise D for Part 2, Chapters 12–13 (p. 64)
Research

Answers will vary.

Review Exercise F for Part 2, Chapters 16 (p. 66)
MLA Documentation

O'Neill, Terry. Introduction. <u>Censorship: Opposing Viewpoints</u>. St.
Paul: Greenhaven, 1985. 13–14.
Hentoff, Nat. "The Speech Police Invade Cyberspace." <u>Village Voice</u>
11 July 1995: 22–23.

Chapter 19   Exercise B (p. 68)
Sentence Review

Answers will vary.

Chapter 19   Exercise D (p. 70)
Simple Sentences

Answers will vary.

1. X
2. S; Brian
3. X
4. X
5. S; vacation

Chapter 20   Exercise B (p. 72)
Building Complex Sentences

Answers will vary. Possible responses are provided.

1. The coach presented the game ball to Angela, who hit the game-winning home run.
2. Although my best friend is my dog, her best friend is a delicious bone.
3. Because Mr. Adamson Adamson often forgets to record his checks in the checkbook, Mrs. Adamson has learned not to trust him.

Chapter 21   Exercise B (p. 74)
Writing Emphatic Sentences

When the Vikings landed on a European coast, inhabitants learned to fear their sudden and fierce raids. These Norsemen sailed their high-powered boats from Scandinavia to the continent or Britain. They decorated their ships with striped sails and colorful circular shields. These ships brought little brightness to the raiders' victims. The Vikings left a permanent mark on the territories they attacked and occupied with ferocity and persistence. The Vikings' customs and language particularly influenced Norman France and the region of the British "Danelaw."

Chapter 22　　Exercise B (p. 76)
Writing Concise Sentences

The seven daughters of Atlas, known as the Pleiades, were pursued by Orion, who was unable to seize any of them. Orion continued to follow them until Zeus took pity on them and placed them in the heavens. Although seven stars make up the Pleiades constellation, only six stars are clearly visible. The seventh is invisible except to those who have especially keen vision. In Greek mythology, the seventh star represented Electra, mother of Dardanus, who founded the Trojan race. The legend held that, rather than look down upon the destruction of Troy, Electra dropped from the sky. Today, though, with the aid of binoculars, well over seven stars are visible in this cluster. Viewing through a telescope yields several hundred.

Chapter 22　　Exercise D (p. 78)
Writing Concise Sentences

Shakespeare's source for the story of *Macbeth* was Holinshed's *Chronicles*. There he found the account of King Duncan's murder, the suggestion about Lady Macbeth's ambition, and the tale of Macbeth's rise and fall.

Chapter 23　　Exercise B (p. 80)
Writing Varied Sentences

1.　a. One of the more intriguing literary legends surrounding the King James Version of the Bible alleges that Shakespeare's hand is present in the 46th Psalm.

　　b. Turn to the Psalm to see for yourself.

2.　a. Count to the forty-sixth word from the beginning of the psalm (*shake*) and then identify the forty-sixth word from the end of the psalm (*spear*).

　　b. These findings might be dismissed as merely interesting.

3. a. The situation becomes even more intriguing when we realize that Shakespeare was forty-six years old when the revision work was underway in 1610.

b. We shouldn't be surprised to find that Shakespeare played a role in translating this magnificently poetic portion of the King James Version.

One of the more intriguing literary legends surrounding the King James Version of the Bible alleges that Shakespeare's hand is present in the 46th Psalm. Turn to the Psalm to see for yourself. Count to the forty-sixth word from the beginning of the psalm (*shake*) and then identify the forty-sixth word from the end of the psalm (*spear*). These findings might be dismissed as merely interesting coincidence. The situation becomes even more intriguing, however, when we realize that Shakespeare was forty-six years old when the revision was underway in 1610. We shouldn't be surprised to find that Shakespeare played a role in translating this magnificently poetic portion of the King James Version.

Chapter 23   Exercise D (p. 82)
Writing Varied Sentences

Giorgio Vasari, the Italian art historian who lived during the sixteenth century, records an interesting anecdote concerning Leonardo's use of models. For his models of the disciples, Leonardo drew from life, encountering difficulty only in locating a suitable Judas Iscariot. Throughout much of his work on the painting, Leonardo was troubled by the prior of Santa Maria, who monitored the work's progress from a vantage uncomfortably close for the artist. Upon hearing that the prior had expressed his concerns to Duke Sforza, Leonardo mentioned that any delay he had experienced was merely the result of his having encountered difficulty in identifying a model for the betrayer. But, Leonardo pointed out, he would be delayed no longer, for he had located his model: the prior would serve nicely.

Review Exercise B for Part 3, Chapters 19–23 (p. 84)
Sentence Style

Answers will vary. One possible response follows.

I skied about twenty feet at a time and then I stopped so I would not pick up too much momentum. This process continued with healthy results until I reached one particularly demanding part of the slope. It consisted of a sharp drop, followed by a ninety-degree turn. I was looking at a deathtrap waiting to engulf me. I said a quick prayer and pushed off, not knowing what lay ahead.

I handled the steep drop with minimal effort, but my luck ran out as I attempted to turn. I tried to maneuver around an unsuspecting skier and lost control. Instead of turning, I veered off the ski trail. Of course, I collided with the poor man and bent his ski poles, but this seemed trivial to me as I swiftly headed over the side of the cliff. In mid-air for a few seconds, I rushed head-on into a gate.

For a few seconds, I lay there in the snow, stunned, not realizing what had happened. Then, as I heard my friends calling my name and spectators asking if I were alive, I came back to reality. I had risked my life. I had been participating in something most people call a sport. Fortunately, only my pride was bruised, but I will never again slide down mountains on little pieces of wood.

PART 4 SOLVING COMMON SENTENCE PROBLEMS

Chapter 24   Exercise B (p. 86)
Revising Sentence Fragments

When we moved from an apartment to a house, we discovered that we had more belongings than we thought. So much had to be packed, so we used boxes, suitcases, and even large garbage bags. We rented a truck from the local gas station so we could avoid spending the extra money to hire a mover. We certainly put in a full day's work that day. Although the process was long and hard, it was worth it.

Chapter 24   Exercise D (p. 88)
Revising Sentence Fragments

1. Because the officials did not like the thunder that shook the ground and lightning that brightened the sky, the soccer tournament was postponed until Saturday.
2. Erica not only struck out eleven batters, but she also hit two doubles and drove in five runs.
3. Neither the administrators nor the faculty correctly projected enrollment trends.

Chapter 25   Exercise B (p. 90)
Revising Comma Splices and Fused Sentences

1. RO   speak / the
2. RO   letter / another
3. RO   business / everyone
4. RO   small / only
5. C

6. RO   players / Reece
7. RO   deck / his
8. RO   call / has
9. RO   detail / each
10. RO   you / I

Chapter 25   Exercise D (p. 92)
Revising Comma Splices and Fused Sentences

Cats make great pets, but you have to be affectionate with them. As they are rather independent animals, they do not always come when you call them. Many people prefer dogs because you can train them to come or sit or fetch a bone. With cats, on the other hand, you have to be willing to let them live their own lives. If you attempt to train them, you may become discouraged. If you put two cats in the same room, you are in for quite a treat. They chase each other, usually all in fun. When one catches the other, the real show begins. Often they will cuddle and clean each other, but sometimes they will fight. The wise pet owner will know when to break up a fight and when to let it go, because it is only play for the cats. They can be great company if you understand them.

Chapter 26   Exercise B (p. 94)
Revising Faulty Modification

1. Although a small part of the world's population, people in developed countries are using up proportionally more of the earth's nonrenewable natural resources.
2. As fossil fuels, minerals, metals, timber, and water are diminishing, they cannot be replaced because they were built up over billions of years.
3. With the doubling of the world consumption of oil every decade, time would seem short for a change.
4. When certain coastal areas are flooded, such minerals as common salt, magnesium, and bromine can be extracted from seawater through evaporation.
5. According to experts, one-half to one-third of the world's additional energy needs in the next twenty years will be satisfied by the use of coal, although it pollutes the atmosphere.

Chapter 26   Exercise D (p. 96)
Revising Faulty Modification

On arriving in America, Pierre was amazed by the sights and sounds. Because he traveled alone, the sight of so many people hurrying around and shouting came as a jolt to him. Coming from a small village in the south of France, the young traveler had never before witnessed so much commotion. He was only eight years old and a bit nervous, and his luggage seemed to be his only companion. On this trip, his cousins in Philadelphia would be his hosts. Looking for them at the gate, he was not able to find them. Then an attendant took him to the information booth and paged his cousins over the loudspeaker. To locate them, the attendant had to make an announcement twice. Then Pierre recognized his relatives running through the terminal, from the other end of the building. Feeling relieved, Pierre ran to them and escaped the crazy crowds of America.

Chapter 27   Exercise B (p. 98)
Revising Faulty Parallelism

(The location of the answers will vary.)

1. a. Amy Rohling, one of the most talented people we know, is a painter, an actress, and a playwright.
   b. Amy Rohling, one of the most talented people we know, paints, acts, and writes plays.

2. a. The camera takes clear pictures and is easy to use.
   b. It is a camera that takes clear pictures and is easy to use.

3. a. Megan Nelson manages to hold a responsible position, to earn an impressive salary, and to write a novel.
   b. Megan Nelson is holding a responsible position, earning an impressive salary, and writing a novel.

4. a. In the recording of popular music, the separate tasks necessary to produce, to arrange, and to engineer are often performed by one person who is called the producer.
   b. In the recording of popular music, the separate tasks of producing, arranging, and engineering are often performed by one person who is called the producer.

5. a. When we are well rehearsed, when our timing is precise, and when our singer is in good voice, we sound as good as any other band in the city.
   b. When we are well rehearsed, our timing is precise, and our singer is in good voice, we sound as good as any other band in the city.

6. a. On their first date, they were talking, eating, and drinking for hours after most others had left.
   b. On their first date, they talked, ate, and drank for hours after most others had left.

7. a. Laura refuses either to go by bus or to ride the subway.
   b. Laura refuses to go by bus or by subway.

8. a. Are marrying, child-rearing, and shopping all there is to life after graduate school?
   b. Are to marry, to rear children, and to shop all there is to life after graduate school?

9. a. At thirteen months, my grandson Michael exhibits remarkable agility of movement, comprehends complex ideas, and shows aggressiveness of character.
   b. At thirteen months, my grandson Michael exhibits remarkable agility of movement, comprehension of complex ideas, and aggressiveness of character.

Chapter 27 Exercise D (p. 100)
Revising Faulty Parallelism

For hundreds and thousands of years, the Nile Valley experienced an annual flood. The Nile's floodwaters carried soil particles from upstream, deposited them throughout the flood plain, and renewed the fertility of the Egyptian fields. Although it might be interpreted as a natural disaster, the yearly event permitted the rise of one of the richest and most advanced ancient civilizations. The flood enabled the people to grow enough food to support a large population, allowing time for other activities, including building, scholarship, and art.

During the past century, construction of the Aswan High Dam has brought enormous changes to the Nile Valley. The dam is designed to retain an entire annual flow of the Nile and provide power to make cheap fertilizers, which are needed by the intensively cultivated farms that are no longer covered by silty Nile water. The dam has ended the Nile Valley's annual flood, which used to bring the region nutritious silt that was once cherished for its nutrients. Many people now consider the silt a nuisance because it fills up irrigation canals.

Chapter 28 Exercise B (p. 102)
Revising Awkward or Confusing Sentences

1. close; need
   closed, needed
2. wants; dreads
   wanted; dreaded
3. stay; pay
   stayed; paid
4. washed; began
   washes; begin
5. runs; hopes
   ran; hoped

Chapter 28   Exercise D (p. 104)
Revising Awkward or Confusing Sentences

I work in a bank, and when one has that type of job, he has to be willing to wake up at a very early hour. Each morning, I drive to work, park my car, and walk a block to work. I get a lunch break every day at noon, and I love to eat at the delicatessen around the corner. I had worked at the bank for over a year, and decided that I had had enough. After looking around for a new job, I found one where I had to be at work at 6:00 a.m. This job was in a restaurant where I had to stand up all day, and after six months, I decided to go back to the bank. The manager was very nice to me and said, "You can have your old job back if you promise to stay at least two years." I took the job, and I now enjoy an extra hour of sleep every morning.

Review Exercise B for Part 4, Chapters 24–28 (p. 107)
Solving Common Sentence Problems

Making Waffles

After a long night's sleep, how would you like to sit down to a cup of hot coffee and golden brown waffles for breakfast? You would probably like them with warm strawberries and a scoop of fresh, whipped cream, or you might prefer the traditional butter and maple syrup. In any case, waffles are an excellent breakfast dish, for they are easy to prepare, and there are many ways to serve them. Basically, making waffles involves three steps: preparing the batter, cooking the waffle, and deciding how to top it.

First, before mixing the batter, it is a good idea to preheat the waffle iron. Most irons have to be plugged in, and usually take from ten to fifteen minutes to heat up. I have found that medium is usually the best setting, but you'll have to decide which setting works best for you.

Mixing the batter is a relatively simple task. First, combine the following in a large mixing bowl: one cup cake flour, two tablespoons of sugar, two teaspoons of baking powder, and one-fourth teaspoon of salt.

Next, add one cup of milk and one tablespoon of vegetable oil to the dry ingredients. It is important to add the oil to the batter; otherwise, the waffles will stick to the iron. If you don't have any vegetable oil, one tablespoon of melted butter or margarine will suffice. Use a medium-sized spoon to stir the batter until it forms a smooth mixture without any lumps in it.

After thoroughly stirring the batter, making sure that there aren't any lumps in it, crack two eggs into a small bowl. Take care not to break the yolks, and make sure that there aren't any pieces of shell in the bowl.

Next, separate the yolks with a small spoon, and store them in an appropriate container, since they will not be added to the batter. Use a small fork to beat the egg whites until they become frothy. Then, combine the egg whites with the batter, mixing them in completely. Preparing the egg whites in this manner seems like a waste of time when you could just toss them into the batter. But this way, the waffles turn out with a light, fluffy texture on the inside.

By this time, the waffle iron is probably finished preheating. Use the mixing spoon to put some batter in the waffle iron, filling all of the ridges of the iron's bottom side. Now, use a low, medium, or high setting to cook the waffle to your desired preference, golden brown, or for some, burned. Following these instructions will produce four medium-sized waffles.

Finally, the hardest part of preparing waffles is deciding what topping to use. Whatever topping you decide to use—fruit and cream, butter and syrup, or even ice cream—waffles are always a special as well as a splendid addition to anyone's breakfast menu. Try them sometime.

PART 5 USING WORDS EFFECTIVELY

Chapter 29   Exercise B (p. 110)
Choosing Words

Answers will vary.

Chapter 29   Exercise D (p. 112)
Choosing Words

Answers will vary.

Chapter 30   Exercise B (p. 114)
Using a Dictionary

(Using *American Heritage Dictionary*, 3rd edition)

1.   fast, faster, fastest

airy, airier, airiest
mere, no comparative, merest
homey, homier, homiest
unlucky, unluckier, unluckiest

2. become: both
    elect: both
    find: both
    give: both

Chapter 30   Exercise D (p. 116)
Using a Dictionary

(Using *American Heritage Dictionary*, 3rd edition)

1. 1978
2. George Washington Gale Ferris, 1859-1896
3. 32.064
4. Jean Baptiste Poquelin
5. A twentieth-century literary and artistic movement that attempts to express the workings of the subconscious and is characterized by fantastic imagery and incongruous juxtaposition of subject matter

Chapter 31   Exercise B (p. 118)
Improving Spelling

1. accept
2. affected
3. capital
4. lie
5. there
6. exception
7. lose
8. license
9. Driving
10. already
11. possession
12. friendly

Review Exercise B for Part 5, Chapters 29–31 (p. 121)
Using Words Effectively

[Note: Students may revise this essay in a variety of ways. The following serves as one example of effective revision. Pilot Mountain, North Carolina, may be better known to your students as Mount Pilot, a town near Mayberry on "The Andy Griffith Show."]

Pilot Mountain

Towering above the foothills, enveloped in blankets of vibrant emerald pines and maples, lies my precious landmark, overshadowing the mere human creations at its giant feet. This colossus has a peculiar shape, as if God took His chisel and hand-carved each unique rock formation. Nowhere else on earth is there another such creation.

The best way to see the formation is from the second highest point on the mountain, known as the Little Pinnacle. To reach this spot, one must scale sharp, huge rocks; avoid steep, dangerous edges; and evade large, bulky trees. After the strenuous hike, one can rest upon any of the numerous, large rocks at the top of the Little Pinnacle and gaze upon the most famous point on the mountain: the Knob.

The Knob is perfectly rounded, with natural stone walls descending from its top. No vegetation grows on the walls. Thus, the tall pine trees rising from the top create an almost comical flattop hairstyle. On clear days, the Knob is visible from sixty miles away. From any point, it presents a remarkable sight, but the view from the Little Pinnacle is still the best.

PART 6 UNDERSTANDING GRAMMAR

Chapter 32   Exercise B (p. 124)
Parts of Speech: Pronouns

1. me
2. their
3. we
4. its
5. I
6. Who
7. Whom
8. whom
9. I
10. me
11. us
12. He
13. me
14. she
15. me

Chapter 32   Exercise D (p. 126)
Parts of Speech: Verbs

1. C	6. I	11. I
2. I	7. C	12. C
3. C	8. I	13. I
4. I	9. I	14. C
5. C	10. I	15. I

Chapter 32   Exercise F (p. 128)
Parts of Speech: Adjectives

1. curly	9. their
2. a	10. Both
3. tired	11. Each
4. sloppy	12. This
5. unsightly	13. These
6. lucky	14. tense
7. golden	15. a
8. sweet	

Chapter 32   Exercise H (p. 130)
Parts of Speech: Adverbs

1. gently	9. slowly
2. carefully	10. fast
3. seldom	11. gracefully
4. perfectly	12. wildly
5. manfully	13. often
6. usually	14. more loudly
7. rarely	15. last
8. highly	

Chapter 32   Exercise J (p. 132)
Parts of Speech: Prepositions

1. to	6. Between
2. in spite of	7. behind
3. across	8. among
4. above	9. toward
5. Before	10. before

Chapter 32 Exercise L (p. 134)
Parts of Speech: Prepositions

1. During	6. with
2. On	7. of
3. at	8. into
4. against	9. In
5. under	10. On

Chapter 32 Exercise N (p. 136)
Parts of Speech: Conjunctions

1. Since	6. for example
2. and	7. or
3. While	8. nor
4. because	9. although
5. nevertheless	10. unless

Chapter 32 Exercise P (p. 138)
Parts of Speech: Interjections

1. Wow
2. Ouch
3. Oh
4. Heavens

Chapter 33 Exercise B (p. 140)
Nouns and Pronouns

1. X, they're
2. X, Their
3. X, Who's
4. X, Whose
5. X, women's

Chapter 33   Exercise D (p. 142)
Nouns and Pronouns

Answers will vary.

Chapter 33   Exercise F (p. 144)
Nouns and Pronouns

1. their
2. Whose
3. its
4. It's
5. your
6. their
7. Who's
8. governor's
9. Women's
10. your

Chapter 34   Exercise B (p. 146)
Verbs

1. moved
2. knit, sew
3. were
4. could light
5. sputter, flicker, drip
6. wrote
7. did write
8. will be responsible
9. should be used
10. will bring
11. visited
12. hopes
13. could have served
14. has crashed
15. would prefer
16. has been seen

Chapter 34   Exercise D (p. 148)
Verbs

1. escorted, to take, are waiting [or will wait]
2. began
3. had listened
4. sat
5. broke

Chapter 35   Exercise B (p. 150)
Agreement

1. The subject *he* (singular) agrees with the verb *fishes*; the subject Mr. Mims (singular although it ends in *s*) agrees with the verb *comes*;
2. the subject *he* (singular) agrees with the verb *considers*. *Every* (singular) serves as the subject for the verb *was*; the subject *thunderstorm* agrees with the verb *passed*.
3. The subject *Aerodynamics* (singular although it ends in *s*) agrees with the verb *is*.

Chapter 35   Exercise D (p. 152)
Agreement

Carpenters use many different tools in their work. When they are faced with jobs that are particularly difficult, they have to use their patience as well as their skills. Without patience, hammers, saws, or screwdrivers will do carpenters no good. They have to be able to understand the problems, and find the best ways to solve them. Sometimes, the quickest solutions are not the best. Their customers, or clients, have to be pleased with their work, or they lose their chances to be hired for other jobs. There are great pressures on carpenters to succeed. By no means are their jobs easy.

Chapter 35   Exercise F (p. 154)
Agreement

1. their
2. his
3. its
4. her
5. its
6. its
7. his
8. his
9. his
10. their

Chapter 36   Exercise B (p. 156)
Adjectives and Adverbs

1. unique
2. more delicate
3. more sick
4. taller
5. heavier
6. heaviest
7. grateful
8. youngest
9. faster
10. worse

Review Exercise B for Part 6, Chapters 32–36 (p. 159)
Understanding Grammar

[Note: Students may revise this essay in a variety of ways. The following is one example of effective revision.]

Mocha the Wonder Dog

On April 6, 1990, Mocha, my cocker spaniel, was born. Six months following her birth, I began to train Mocha with Mr. Cowart, a professional dog trainer. After two weeks of obedience training, Mocha learned the "Heel" and "Sit" commands. We worked for four more weeks, spending thirty minutes a day on more basic obedience commands. Mocha, of course, responds very well. Not only did she learn all of the obedience commands, but she and I also built a strong relationship. We were best friends.

I felt good about what I had done with Mocha and how she had learned all of those obedience commands. Mocha and I continued to work with one another even after the classes ended. During that time, she started doing things that I had nothing to do with. For some reason, she liked to chase cars that drove on the street in front of our house.

On a hot summer day, a tragedy happened. My father drove a different truck down our driveway. Mocha hadn't really recognized who was driving the truck or the truck itself, so she darted in front of the truck, trying to make it slow down before entering the yard. Unfortunately, the right front wheel hit Mocha in the hind leg, and the right back wheel hit her in the head.

Fortunately, Mocha was still alive! She didn't allow anyone but me to help her. Scared to death, I picked her up and put her in the back of the truck. My dad rushed Mocha and me to the animal hospital. Mocha's blood was all over my hands and shirt, but I didn't care. All I wanted was for Mocha to have the best medical care possible. Nearly crying, I lifted Mocha from the truck and took her inside the animal hospital.

After four days of treatment, the veterinarians allowed me to take Mocha home, provided that I kept her under close supervision. Limping away from the veterinarians, Mocha was eager to go home. Another two weeks passed before she had totally healed. After Mocha had recovered, we continued her training, and she has made even more astonishing accomplishments. I am so proud of Mocha! Now that I am in college, I miss her very much, but I will see her again when I go home.

PART 7 UNDERSTANDING PUNCTUATION AND MECHANICS

Chapter 37   Exercise B (p. 162)
Using End Punctuation

1. Supreme Court Justice Sample's speech at the A.B.A. convention was scheduled for 10 a.m., but it was postponed until 2 p.m.
2. This CD-ROM has more memory than all the RAM that was on the first computer that I owned.
3. After Beth graduated from FSU with a J.D., she interviewed with NASA in Florida and with the JPL in California.

Chapter 37   Exercise D (p. 164)
Using End Punctuation

1. Are you kidding? I never said that.
2. Caught up in the excitement of the game, the announcer shouted, "What a spectacular shot!"
3. Wow! Just what I always wanted! A red Mustang!

Chapter 38   Exercise B (p. 166)
Using Commas

1. Monet, Renoir, Degas,
2. Angela, our most skillful speakers,
3. newspaper,`
4. Slowly, slyly, and cautiously,
5. school, *It, Caesar, Juliet,*
7. that,
10. elephant, performer,

Chapter 38   Exercise D (p. 168)
Using Commas

1. wand,	6. week,
2. Never, never	7. answer, wrong,
3. bacon, lettuce,	8. (no comma)
4. Who, opinion,	9. 18,
5. (no comma)	10. arrived,

244

Chapter 39   Exercise B (p. 170)
Using Semicolons

1. Television soap operas provide a diversion to real life; their characters are often wealthy and never seem to work.
2. Ads on afternoon soap operas are directed primarily toward women and rarely at men; these ads for women include soap, toothpaste, skin creams, and nail products.

Chapter 39   Exercise D (p. 172)
Using Semicolons

1. Research on animals' ability to think has been conducted on dolphins, who often respond to communicative gestures; sea lions, who seem to show some understanding of logical relationships between symbols; and parrots, who can be taught vocabulary.
2. Through his computer-enhanced classroom lectures, Dr. Riser took his students around the world: they visited the pyramids of Giza, guarded by the Sphinx; they climbed the Acropolis, where they walked among the Parthenon's ruins; and they heard the choirs of the Gothic cathedrals, including Chartres and Lyon.

Chapter 40   Exercise B (p. 174)
Using Apostrophes

1. I'm, can't
2. child's, '76
3. bachelor's, country's
4. Y's, N's
5. Ooh's, ah's
6. hour's, day's
7. yes's, maybe's
8. ABC's
9. Cowarts'
10. Amy's, Jessica's
11. '73
12. partners'
13. She's, he's, children's
14. we'll, we're

Chapter 41   Exercise B (p. 176)
Using Quotation Marks

1. "Why in the world," asked Amanda in her customary frantic manner, "would you think that I'm annoyed by the dent that suddenly appeared in the fender?"
2. To many freshmen, "social security" means a date for Saturday night.
3. Christopher Marlowe posed this question about Helen of Troy: "Was this the face that launched a thousand ships, / And burnt the topless towers of Ilium?"
4. *Aggravate* means "to worsen," while *irritate* means "to annoy."
5. "If you'll submit your research paper one week early," announced Professor Davis, "I'll give you ten percent extra credit, and you won't have to take the term examination."

Chapter 42   Exercise B (p. 178)
Using Other Punctuation Marks

trouble;
discussed:
achievements;
games;
newspapers;

Chapter 42 Exercise D (p. 180)
Using Other Punctuation Marks

1. George Orwell's *1984* (1949) focuses on the dangers of a totalitarian society.
2. The final score (56-0) was a devastating blow for the Wildcats.
3. Hoyt told us that Belize (formerly British Honduras) offers spectacular off-shore diving opportunities.
4. The first phonics book (*Phonics Is Fun*) has a bright blue cover.
5. Some high school students participate in so many extracurricular activities (band, sports, drama club, and school newspaper, for instance) that they have little time to study.

Chapter 43 Exercise B (p. 182)
Capitalization

1. fall, Angela, Erica, Beth, Brian, Halloween
2. Maple Street, highway, north, Cumberland State Park
3. Andrew Luke Thomas, Buddha, Buddhism, India
4. Americans, Roaring Twenties, Great Depression
5. George Elliot's *Middlemarch*
6. Mayflower Compact, Plymouth Colony
7. summer, Big Dipper

Chapter 44 Exercise B (p. 184)
Italics

1. schism
2. there, their
3. strombis pugilis
4. Los Angeles Times, Newsweek
5. Sixteenth Century Journal
6. Renaissance Studies
7. Mayflower
8. canteen, cantina
9. Ailuropoda melanoleuca
10. Messiah

Chapter 45   Exercise B (p. 186)
Hyphens

1. My pre-certification class has fifty-three students on the roster, but only thirty-seven have shown up.
2. By emphasizing her position as a middle-of-the-road independent, the little-known candidate hopes to win the runoff.
3. One of the restaurant's blue-plate specials is chicken-fried steak.
4. Both Texas and Virginia are right-to-work states.
5. Don stood on tiptoe to see the near-perfect statue, which was well-hidden by the security fence.
6. The new store in the mall has a self-service makeup counter and stocks many up-to-the-minute gadgets.
7. The so-called Saturday night special is opposed by pro-gun control groups.
8. For his pre-game meal, he ordered two all-beef patties with special sauce, lettuce, cheese, pickles, and onions on a sesame seed bun.
9. Although last night's speaker presented some thought-provoking insights, he hardly presented any earth-shattering conclusions.
10. The Braves-Mets game was rained out, so the long-suffering fans left for home.

Chapter 46   Exercise B (p. 188)
Abbreviations

1. St., throughout, February
2. eastern standard time, mountain standard time
3. Master of Arts, junior college, university, Tennessee
4. Introduction, Monday, Wednesday, and, Friday, Building
5. anthropology, literature, Christmas, afternoon

Chapter 47   Exercise B (p. 190)
Numbers

1. 12, 16-B, 75
2. June 8, 1985, $547
3. seven
4. 9 a.m. (or 9:00 a.m.)
5. 9, 22
6. Seventeenth, one o'clock, 6

Review Exercise B for Part 7, Chapters 37–42 (p. 192)
Understanding Punctuation

Small towns and cities, especially older ones, face difficult financial problems. Their revenues are limited, but they're expected to maintain service levels, despite added costs. Sometimes the size of a town's annual budget is restricted by the state; in other cases, the local officials determine its size. Ultimately, such budgets are limited by the ability and willingness of citizens to pay the property taxes that generally fund such municipalities.

When a municipal budget is strained, officials have two choices: increase revenues or cut expenditures. In the past, extra funds came from the state and federal governments, but now many towns must do without such aid. Instead, increased revenues can come only from new homes (whose owners pay property taxes), new or revitalized businesses (whose tax bills rise with their revenues), or new industry (whose taxes are a function of space occupied and revenues).

In an older town, however, with little vacant land, not much new growth can be encouraged. In addition, revitalizing an old, run-down business district requires time, capital, and community support. Thus, if revenues can't or don't grow, towns have no choice but to cut their expenses.

How can a town or small city spend less? One city manager summed up the problem when he said, "We're like a business during tough times. We have to be more efficient, more careful with our pennies, and more concerned about our customers—the demanding, overburdened taxpayers who depend on our services." And how does a town accomplish this? Few communities have long-term answers, for many fixed costs—pensions, utilities, insurance, and the like—are beyond their control.

Review Exercise D for Part 7, Chapters 43–47 (p. 195)
Spelling and Mechanics

1. Although the calendar said January, it was a surprisingly warm, spring-like Thursday morning—January 28th, to be exact—and all Andrew could think about was how he would celebrate his birthday with his brothers.
2. Luke earned a four-year scholarship to the Florida public college of his choice; his goal is to earn an M.A. and then choose a graduate school where he can earn a doctorate.

3. One of the most famous of eighteenth-century literary pieces is Jonathan Swift's *Gulliver's Travels*, which we read in our English 2210 class last semester.
4. The local teachers' union negotiated an excellent contract; each teacher will have twenty-seven paid holidays—including two weeks during the Christmas break; one week for the Easter break; and her birthday, plus the day before and the day after.

PART 8 WRITING IN THE DISCIPLINES

Chapter 48   Exercise B (p. 198)
Understanding the Disciplines

Answers will vary.

Chapter 49   Exercise B (p. 200)
Writing in the Humanities

Answers will vary.

Chapter 50   Exercise B (p. 202)
Writing in the Social Sciences

Answers will vary.

Chapter 51   Exercise B (p. 204)
Writing in the Natural and Applied Sciences

Answers will vary.

Chapter 52   Exercise B (p. 206)
Writing Essay Exams

Answers will vary.

Chapter 53 Exercise B (p. 208)
Writing about Literature

Answers will vary.

Chapter 54 Exercise B (p. 211)
Writing for the Workplace

Answers will vary.

Chapter 55 Exercise B (p. 214)
Document Design and Manuscript Format

Answers will vary.

Review Exercise B for Part 8, Chapters 48–53 (p. 216)
Writing in the Disciplines

Answers will vary.

PART 9 ESL AND GLOSSARIES

Chapter 56 Exercise B (p. 218)
ESL: Language Issues for International Students

Answers will vary.

Chapter 57 Exercise B (p. 220)
A Glossary of Usage

1. accept
2. effect
3. Whose
4. allusion
5. It's

6. your
7. their
8. among
9. complimented
10. conscious